The Forest AND the Trees

The Forest AND the Trees

Helping Readers Identify Important
Details in Texts and Tests
Grades 4–8

Emily Kissner

HEINEMANN
Portsmouth, NH

Heinemann
361 Hanover Street
Portsmouth, NH 03801–3912
www.heinemann.com

Offices and agents throughout the world

Library of Congress Cataloging-in-Publication Data
Kissner, Emily.
 The forest and the trees : helping readers identify important details in texts and tests, grades 4–8 / Emily Kissner.
  p. cm.
 Includes bibliographical references.
 ISBN-13: 978-0-325-01195-0
 ISBN-10: 0-325-01195-8
 1. Reading comprehension—Study and teaching. 2. Content area reading. I. Title.
 LB1050.45.K464 2008
 428.4'3—dc22   2008020810

Editor: Lisa Luedeke
Production editor: Sonja S. Chapman
Cover design: Lisa Fowler
Compositor: Eric Rosenbloom, Kirby Mountain Composition
Manufacturing: Valerie Cooper

Printed in the United States of America on acid-free paper

12 11 10 09 08 PAH 1 2 3 4 5

Contents

Acknowledgments

Turning the dynamic work of the classroom into words on a page is a challenging task. There are many people who have aided me along the way, from helping me to think through concepts to encouraging me to even commit my ideas to paper.

Many of the ideas in this book began as conversations that I had with my husband, Steve Kissner, as we drove back and forth to school. My husband's probing questions and careful analysis helped me clarify and refine my thinking. Even more important, his support enabled me to take the leap to do more research and get started with writing. It is not an exaggeration to say that this book is as much his as mine.

I would also like to thank the dedicated colleagues who have helped and supported me throughout the writing of this book. Megan McLean, Nicole King, Michele Sokol, Cyndi Smith, Pam Tate, and Colleen Smith all tried activities from this book in their own classrooms and gave me valuable insights into what worked and what didn't.

My mother, Karen Pearce, gave me important information about how the activities worked with eighth graders. She also offered tremendous support to our entire family through the writing of this book. I'd also like to thank my brother, Will Pearce, for writing the best subject lines ever seen in email and helping me to learn how to pay attention to details from a very early age. My sister, Sarah Hopper, has always noticed the little details of life and has helped to clue me in to some very important ideas.

My son Zachary has also been an important help. As I wrote stories and activities, he tested them and offered me ideas. It's been a delight to watch his ability to make inferences and visualize unfold. My younger son, Aidan, has taught me in a different way, proving that a toddler will always manage to find the Caps Lock button on a keyboard. Aidan's ability to find the details that matter to him led me to thinking about how we develop the ability to think about details at all.

I would also like to acknowledge the support of some of the people that I have gotten to know at Bendersville Elementary over the past few months. Colleen Smith and Kaye Boyer, as well as Annie Granger and Shane Brewer, have been very welcoming. I'd like to thank the administrators from the Upper Adams School District, including Ann Wolfe, Eric Eschbach, and Mary Paxton, for their continued support.

The sixth-grade students I taught in 2006–2007 will always have a special place in my heart. Their positive energy and their enthusiasm for learning made every day of teaching a delight. From the palm tree named Kevin to the daily dramas of friendships, they kept life interesting.

It's a little intimidating for a teacher to reach out to the world of academic research. However, I always received the most gracious responses from my correspondents. I'd like to thank Rebecca Fincher-Kiefer and Jeffrey Walczyk for their kindness in answering my questions and helping me understand some deeper matters of reading.

I'd also like to thank everyone at Heinemann, especially Kate Montgomery, Heather Anderson, and Lisa Luedeke. Heather has offered wonderful feedback and helped me find the vision for this book, keeping up my spirits as I faced a change of grade level and school.

SEEING THE FOREST *AND* THE TREES

1

Details are the bane of my existence. Each day a new pack of them howls outside my classroom door, waiting to tear me to shreds. Who needs to bring in lunch money. Who needs to go to band, and when. Which papers I need to fill out for IEPs, 504 plans, and my certification. Who to mark absent, who will go to the office to do the announcements, who turned in homework, who did not turn in homework, who needs to go to the guidance counselor. No matter how hard I try to tame these details, at least one will escape to bare its teeth, growl, and bite me.

But at the same time I am trying to escape these rabid details, I actually invite other details into the classroom. "Remember to use text-based details to support your responses," I tell students while we practice writing short-answer responses for state tests. "Let's categorize these details from the story based on whether they are relevant or irrelevant," I tell a reading group. "Wow! I love the detail in your drawing!" I say, looking at a marvelously intricate picture of a dragon that a student drew during indoor recess.

I became interested in the role that details play in my classroom as I was teaching summarizing. I saw that students had trouble deciding which details to include in their summaries. Which were the important details? How did they relate to the main ideas? Which details were interesting, but not important?

I have to admit that my own inclination is to let details slide. Given a choice between focusing on details or main ideas, I will choose the main ideas every time. After all, I wrote a book about summarizing. But I owed it to my students to cast aside my doubts about details and learn more. I wanted to know how students used details to form inferences, visualize, and learn new information.

The more attention I paid to how my students processed details, the more I noticed that not all details are the same. There are details in the text, but there are also details that students have in their prior knowledge. These details can interact to shape comprehension. If a student misses an important detail, she can fail to make an important inference or grasp the main idea of a passage.

But other details can pull a reader away from a text. These might be the interesting, seductive details that authors use to make their writing

more interesting or they might be details from the student's prior knowledge that contradict the author's main ideas. In order to help students
make sense of these different details, I would need to show them how to
notice the details of the world around them, how to use details to build
inferences, and how to learn from details.

The shadow of state testing, which looms menacingly over my
school year, added another wrinkle to my work with details. Not only
would I need to help students understand different kinds of details in text,
but I would also need to make sure that they could deal with the details of
standardized tests. Answering multiple-choice questions and writing short
constructed responses are other challenges for students, challenges that
require them to move seamlessly between looking at details and looking at
main ideas.

Over the course of several years, I learned as much as I could about
how readers process details. I'd notice a problem in my students' comprehension, turn to the research journals to figure out what was going on,
and then try to devise ways to help students overcome the problem. In
the busy laboratory of the classroom, I was quickly able to find out what
worked and what didn't.

Big Ideas About Little Details
After two years of scribbling notes about student progress and poring over
student work, I gained a new appreciation for details. And I realized that
just as I wanted students to pay attention to the details in text, I needed to
attend to the details in my classroom. By studying my students' responses
and thinking about their comments, I was able to build some broad generalizations to guide my instruction. Each of these ideas is discussed in
further—well, detail—in later chapters.

- Helping students notice details in real life will build their
  understanding of details in the text.

- Simple classroom assessments can help me to see how my
  students process details.

- Readers process text—and details—in three different ways
  during reading.

- There are many different kinds of inferences. Text-based inferences depend on critical facts from the text, and reader-based
  inferences depend on details in the reader's prior knowledge.

- Visualizing is a form of extended inference.

- The details in expository text present new challenges for young
  readers.

- Prior knowledge can help a reader understand a text but can also interfere with understanding.

- A reader's goals influence what a reader learns from a text.

- Many students don't know how to use specific text details to support a constructed response.

What I learned—from the work of other teachers, from research journals, and from the students themselves—has changed my instruction in unexpected ways. I used to be content to just let details slip through my fingers as I reached for big ideas; now I understand that I need to take the time to notice these little bits of information. Whether I am helping students understand the one word that changes the meaning of a sentence, the one idea that creates the visual image, or the new concept that contradicts prior knowledge, paying attention to the details can have huge rewards.

I still try to get the big picture, to see the whole forest. For a reading teacher, this means that I am essentially trying to get kids to understand what they read. But I have learned to appreciate the different trees in the forest—the many tools and strategies that readers use to get to a deep understanding.

2 BUILDING A BRIDGE
TO DETAILS

After spending a summer as a camp naturalist, I found that I was suddenly noticing hawks. Along highways, at the edges of farm fields, on telephone wires, there they sat, red-tailed hawks and kestrels, watching and brooding. I was astonished at how suddenly they appeared. Had the hawks suddenly appeared out of nowhere? No, there was no surge in hawk numbers. The difference was that now I was looking for them. Something interesting happens when we start looking for details. We see them, in greater richness and clarity than ever before.

Before our students can come to a full awareness of text details, they need to be able to see details in their own lives. Some students, of course, are adept at this. These are the students who bring in intricately designed Lego creations and draw detailed fantasy worlds. But in every classroom, there are the students who have gotten used to living in a world of generalities, a world in which they remember a general statement or idea about an experience but not the details that led them to the generalization.

I noticed this when I asked students to write about their hopes for sixth grade. Hunter wrote, "I know that sixth grade will be fun. I am hoping to have lots of good times in sixth grade. That's why I think it will be fun."

"Why do you think sixth grade will be fun?" I asked Hunter.

"Because it will be. It looked like you guys did fun stuff last year," Hunter answered. The fifth-grade classrooms were right across the hall from ours, so I was expecting incoming sixth-graders like Hunter to have some ideas about what to expect in sixth grade.

"What are some fun things that you're looking forward to?" I asked. I was trying to fish a detail out of Hunter, something specific to anchor his paragraph.

Hunter shrugged. "It's going to be fun. That's all I know."

Hunter's responses were fascinating to me. In his writing, he produced generalizations—*sixth grade will be fun*—without remembering any of the details that he had used to make that generalization. This is common of many of my students. They seem to drift through a world that is either "fun" or "boring" by turns, rarely pausing to consider the details that led them to these generalizations. I imagine these children with file folders in their brains. They file away all the details of an event or experience like papers in a folder. But once they label the folder, it becomes glued shut. Hunter had labeled sixth grade as "fun" and had no need for more thought on the matter. He either could not or would not open his file folder to examine the details within.

In fact, this problem is why students often forget details from year to year. Although they remember the generalization, they do not recall the facts that led to that generalization (Nuthall 1999b).

As you might imagine, this inability to recognize details carries over from real life into writing and reading. When Hunter spoke about his reading, he could recall important nouns or ideas, especially ones that were featured on the cover of the book, but he could not produce the names of characters. His strong compensatory strategies could carry him through a simple narrative, but more sophisticated authorial devices like flashbacks, foreshadowing, and subtle characterization left him stymied. I knew he could do better.

How do I move students like Hunter from a world of generalities into a world of details? I could sit down next to Hunter and point out the details he was missing. This can work in small settings, with carefully controlled text and structured experiences. In the regular classroom, however, this is impractical. Imagine pointing out the details of every independent reading book in a class of twenty-three!

Some teachers I have worked with approach the challenge from a punitive standpoint. From this view, children who do not notice details are being lazy. If we punish them for their laziness—usually by giving them bad grades—then they will learn to not be lazy. Students who have been in this kind of classroom start to think that finding and using details is a tedious, irritating chore, one of those boring things that teachers make students do.

As I have worked with students who show difficulty in recognizing and using details, I've come to a big realization. Before we can be truly successful at helping kids like Hunter notice details in reading, we have to help them observe the details that surround them in real life. Students who are not noticing details in text or producing details in their writing need concrete experiences with details of varying importance. They need repeated opportunities to observe, to talk, to wonder, and to compare. And I have found that one of the best ways to help students notice details is to go where our ability to observe may have begun: outdoors.

Details and the Naturalist Intelligence

Natural experiences are a wonderful way to help sensitize students to details. In fact, our very ability to notice details stems in part from our ability to look at and understand nature. Several years after explaining multiple intelligences, Howard Gardner proposed an eighth intelligence—the naturalist intelligence. People who are strong in this are easily able to recognize similarities and differences, notice patterns and change, and see how items in an environment are connected (Wilson 1998). It's easy to see why the naturalist intelligence is so important for survival. People need this intelligence to be able to tell which plants are poisonous, which clouds produce rain, which places are good for hunting, and which snakes are venomous.

Besides appealing to the naturalist intelligence, taking children outdoors has a wealth of other benefits. Most students find it intrinsically motivating to venture beyond the confines of the school, and they will take more interest in what you do outside. Outdoor trips also have the benefit of adding movement to a lesson, getting kids up and walking around. And going outside will engage students in looking for details that are infinitely more fascinating than what you could produce in the classroom.

For me, our outdoor explorations frame the school year. From the first week of school to the very last day, taking students outside provides an easy way to focus their attention and help them notice details. Although our rambles around the school property may look carefree and leisurely, they are actually the product of careful planning and—of course—attention to detail.

Structuring Outdoor Activities

The prospect of taking students beyond the confining walls of the school can be daunting. Over the years, I've learned that the first step is to explore the school site myself. When I am excited about the location and what we will see, the students can catch some enthusiasm.

But where can we see neat wildlife? Even schoolyards that seem barren and lifeless can yield an interesting array of tiny creatures. I have found that students can be good sources of information. When I taught at a suburban middle school, I was amazed to hear that a few intrepid children had caught crayfish in what I thought was a barren recess yard. A small ditch, actually a buried creek, became the site of one of our first explorations. When I transferred to a rural elementary school, I was thrilled to find an overgrown nature trail beside the school. Kids told me that it had once looped through the wooded area. With the help of a kind custodian, we reclaimed the overgrown path and explored a small forest.

Once I know where to take students, the next challenge is when to go outdoors. Fitting outdoor trips into the school day can be difficult. At Biglerville Elementary, I was fortunate to have a self-contained class, which gave me the flexibility to take forty minutes to an hour for an outdoor experience. When I taught middle school, I did not have the luxury of large blocks of time. To justify our trips outdoors, I made sure that each trip had a clear link to a learning goal or state standard.

After exploring the site and planning for time, I always prepare students for an outdoor trip. The first excursions need to be highly structured, with a clear outcome. This can easily be adjusted depending on your subject area. When I taught just language arts, we would go outdoors to make lists of singular and plural nouns. As I've taught sixth grade, I've linked the first nature trail walk with our study of biotic and abiotic (living and nonliving) components of the ecosystem.

Why not simply say, "We're going outside to look for details"? Of course this is an option. But there are several reasons why I don't generally do this. I don't want to scaffold students to just look for details in isolation, without a meaningful structure to support them. I've also found that loosely structured excursions, especially at the beginning of the year, can lead to misbehavior. The students who don't recognize details, especially those who aren't used to being outside, will simply opt out of the activity and let others do all the noticing and observing.

My trips are more successful when we let the interesting details wiggle in from the sidelines. The goals I set lend themselves to noticing details. However, the details have a home, a conceptual framework in which to live. Over the years, as I've taught different units, I've developed a number of simple ways to structure outdoor trips. These Outdoor Trip Frameworks (Figure 2–1) help me focus students on details.

What I do before we go outdoors has a direct effect on what students get out of the trip. When I have tried to rush through the preparation phase and just get outside, students easily get off task and distracted. The more time I have to spend on management issues while we are outside, the less I am able to help students pay attention to the natural details

---

Outdoor Trip Frameworks

These are some ideas for structuring outdoor trips to help students notice real-life details.

- Make a list of singular and plural nouns.

- List adjectives to describe what you see.

- Find biotic and abiotic components of the ecosystem.

- Sketch a food chain.

- Create a scavenger hunt for younger students.

- Sketch a picture of an object so that someone else will recognize it.

- Find evidence that animals live in an area.

- Write three compound sentences to describe what you see.

FIGURE 2–1.

around them. By taking the time to properly prepare students, we can get to that state of receptive awareness so that students can notice what is around them. Here's how I do it.

1. Brainstorm appropriate behavior for going outdoors. I tell my students they need to "look studious" and emphasize that this is not recess. They enjoy practicing "looking studious" and give me thumbs up or thumbs down as I model various behaviors. I tell students that if they do not behave appropriately, the whole class will return indoors.

2. Discuss the learning goal. I always have students produce some kind of written product—activities like listing and sketching work best. Short outdoor trips do not lend themselves to composing paragraphs or reading lengthy texts.

3. Review what students need to bring with them. They will need clipboards or books to lean on as they write. I've found that old slates work just as well as clipboards, and the students never try to steal them. I always carry several extra pencils, because at least one student inevitably forgets to bring one.

4. Designate and practice a signal, like hand-raising, a whistle, or the call of an owl. I like to practice the signal indoors by telling students to tell a partner something they expect to see, and then giving the signal.

5. Head outdoors!

On this first visit, it's important to be vigilant with behavior and follow through with the promise that students will return indoors if behavior is inappropriate. If students begin to think that outdoor trips are a time to socialize and misbehave, they will not learn what you are trying to teach them. (One class had to return indoors twice before they finally got it together. On the third trip, they were reminding each other of the proper way to behave.)

While on the trip, I stop frequently to allow students time to write. As students stop, I move around the group. My focus is to ask questions and make comments to help students to notice what is around them—the colors, the patterns, the shapes, what is similar and different. The students who love nature tend to gravitate toward me, asking more complex questions. I admit it—it's fun to talk to the children who show an obvious interest in the natural world. I've learned a great deal from these students.

But I can't spend every moment with the nature lovers. Often, I pair them together—"Mark, could you tell Josh about what you noticed?" Then, I go off to the fringes to talk to the students who may not find nature intrinsically motivating. These are the children who need more structured interactions to find the details in nature. I interrupt discussions about shoes or the movies that are coming out over the weekend with a comment about something we've seen. "Candace, did you notice this milkweed? Look at what happens when I pull off a leaf," I say. Or, "Matt and Arturo, did you notice the spittlebug larvae? What does that remind you of?"

Our time outdoors always seems too short. Before we know it, it is time to head back inside. But the experience is far from over. The work I do indoors, after we return, is just as important as what we did outside. First, we always discuss the learning goal of the trip. Then, I build a culture of noticing details. "Did anyone notice anything that surprised you on the trip?" Invariably, students will say that yes, they did see something interesting or unusual.

A classroom chart that we can add to over time is a great way to document what they have seen. I'll often make a heading "What we notice" and another heading "Questions we still have." I model my own questions and observations to get the discussion going. Much of my knowledge of the school site has come from research that we've done after noticing something interesting.

As students become acclimated to the nature experience, their needs change. After three or four trips, they will not need as much structure from you. However, they will begin to request other materials such as field guides, containers to collect creatures, and magnifying glasses. They will ask more interesting questions that show more detailed thinking. By late September, a walk around the meadow loop, which takes fifteen minutes of steady walking, stretches out into a forty-five-minute trek as students stop to examine every interesting detail along the way. They see things that I don't notice—deer tracks, a deer bed, spittlebug egg cases, and even a rabbit skull. One student might ask me to name the different wildflowers—milkweed, ironweed, goldenrod. Another might wonder about the different kinds of birds and which would stay in our area through the winter.

Outdoor activities are one way to help students notice details. These trips motivate students and help them see patterns of similarities and differences. But I have also found that classroom activities can achieve the same kind of results.

Classroom Activities for Developing an Awareness of Details

Details fly fast and furiously through the typical school day—names for different polygons, the parts of an atom, the differences between adjectives and adverbs, when to use a comma and when to use a semicolon. But these are not the only details that stalk the room. There are also the details of who is wearing what and who made comments behind someone else's back at recess. I recognized early on that these details are often more memorable to students than the details of what I am trying to teach.

The Basics of Attention

"Pay attention!" You may find yourself saying this many times a day, hearing this many times a day, or both. Everyone knows what this phrase means, but few stop to consider how silly it sounds. If attention must be paid, then what is the currency?

As it turns out, the currency of attention is energy. Paying attention takes mental energy. How much energy depends on many factors: our interest in the subject, other things that are happening externally, the emotional content of the subject, and so forth. If you have ever felt more tired after a day of faculty meetings than a day of teaching, you have had firsthand experience with the fact that different tasks require different amounts of mental energy.

What are the details that are occupying your attention right now? Given that thousands of different bits of information are bombarding your brain each second, it's pretty amazing that you can focus your attention on anything (Sousa 2001). There are the details from your immediate environment—how hot it is, how your feet feel in your shoes, what other sounds are around you—as well as the details in your brain, such as what memories this text is triggering and what you plan to have for dinner tonight.

The perceptual register is the mechanism that filters all of these different pieces of information and allows the brain to focus. Some researchers also conceptualize an attention-monitoring system with at least three functions: a *selection* system that chooses where to focus attention; a *vigilance* system that maintains the ability to attend, and an *orientation* system that allows a person to change the focus of attention (Posner and Petersen 1990).

To understand the importance of attention in our ability to notice details, we can follow the path of one detail from the environment to the brain. One afternoon, as part of a geometry preassessment, I showed Brad an eight-sided figure and asked, "Is this a quadrilateral?" Brad's first step was to select the number of sides of the polygon as an important feature, and count the sides. But then his attention needed to shift from the external environment to the internal, as he accessed his long-term memory for information that was relevant to the identity of the shape. He needed to remember what the term *quadrilateral* means and whether the shape in front of him was an example of this. Once he determined that the shape was an octagon and not a quadrilateral, he had to shift back from internal to external to make his response.

While this was going on, Brad's attention mechanism still monitored the outside world for other items of importance, ready to shift his attention if necessary. For instance, if the fire alarm had gone off, Brad's attention would have had to shift from the polygon question to the routine for classroom evacuation. In order for Brad to identify a simple polygon, he needed to "pay" attention to the sides, information from his long-term memory, and the people around him. (Sylwester and Cho 1992).

Adding to the burden of attention is the fact that Brad was not looking at the shape in an isolated room. All the hustle and bustle of afternoon choice time was swirling around him. Luckily, our attention mechanism has the ability to distinguish foreground from background and to focus attention on the details in the foreground. Brad decided that the sides of the shape were the foreground details worth noticing at the time and ignored other details that were going on in the room, such as who was wearing a new coat or sporting a new haircut.

You can easily see how one simple conversation takes a great deal of mental energy. When the attention mechanism is working well, then students can notice the important details around them. But there are many pitfalls along the way. Suppose that Brad's attention had been drawn from the shape to the conversations of the people around him. Or suppose that, as he accessed long-term memories about quadrilaterals and geometry, he had gotten lost in remembering fourth grade. When our attention is not focused on the matter at hand, then important details may be lost.

The ability to pay attention can impact a student's ability to understand details. Some students fail to weed out unimportant distractions. Even if they succeed in choosing an appropriate focus for attention, students may find that their attention is pulled away by someone entering the room, a sudden noise, or even a random thought that may or may not be related to the text or the issue at hand. And students may also have trouble changing the focus of attention—for instance, moving from reading a funny story to concentrating on a math problem.

Classroom Activity: The Distraction Game

Many students don't realize that they are in control of their attention. Like captive prisoners of a capricious warden, they allow their attention to flit from place to place, focusing on background details and ignoring what's in the foreground. They fail to notice what is important, or they allow trivial details from their long-term memories to overshadow current conversations.

One spring day, while facing a particularly antsy group of students, I tried to empower them. "You are in charge of your attention," I told them. "You can decide how to focus yourself." This is nothing new to them; they've heard it all year long. "Sometimes it can be difficult to decide what to pay attention to. Here in our classroom, the learning is most important. Even when other things are going on, it's your responsibility to pay attention to the learning." A student stifled a yawn. I needed to think of a quick demonstration. I remembered a segment on the children's television show *Crashbox*, in which a news anchor reads a report while astonishing things happen on the screen. The game is to pay attention to the news report, ignore the silly pictures, and answer the questions correctly. Well, I thought, it was worth a try.

"Today you're going to practice focusing your attention so that you can notice important details. Arturo is going to read this passage aloud." I handed Arturo a short passage related to the next science topic we would be discussing. "While Arturo reads, though, I will be doing my best to distract you. It will be your job to pay attention to Arturo and not to me."

As Arturo started reading, I zoomed through the classroom, making faces, turning off light switches, and tossing a playground ball in the air. Some students giggled, while others looked obviously uncomfortable as they tried to ignore me. Arturo kept reading, even as I turned on the overhead projector, made shadow pictures on the screen, and banged my head in despair as the brand-new bulb burned out. When Arturo finished, I quickly regained my composure and asked the class three questions about the details of what he had just read.

"I didn't hear that part," Abigail admitted when she couldn't answer a question. "You were turning the lights on and off. It was funny."

"I know the answer," Bria spoke up. She added, a little sheepishly, "I had my eyes closed the whole time, so that I could listen to Arturo and not notice what you were doing."

From there, more students spoke up with strategies, difficulties, and ideas. We made the connection between my distracting behaviors and other distractions they might encounter during the school day and how these distractions can grab their attention and cause them to neglect important details.

The Distraction Game is easy to play. First, choose a reading selection that is filled with details. History and science texts work well. Prepare three to five questions based on the text. Because this is a game of attention and not reading comprehension, literal questions with short answers work best.

Then, choose a student to read the passage aloud. To avoid setting dangerous precedents, it's best for the teacher to fill the role of the distractor. At the start of the activity, explain to students that they have control over their attention. They may choose to focus it and direct it as they wish. Then explain the activity. The most important part of this game is the discussion afterward. How did students filter out your distracting behaviors? How did they decide where to focus?

Students like to play Distraction because it makes one of the hardest tasks of school—paying attention—into a game. They also enjoy a chance to see the teacher in a different light. This is a game that engages everyone, from the highly reflective, thoughtful learners to the students who have the most difficulty with attention issues.

Conclusion

When students show that they are unable to locate details in text, or produce details in their writing, one course of action is to take them by the hand and show them the wealth of details that exist in the world around them. By tapping into their naturalist intelligence and learning about the mechanics of attention, students can become attuned to the details around them. Just as I suddenly started to notice hawks, students start to see a world that is rich with delicious details.

In mid-May, after several weeks of bad weather, substitutes, and chorus rehearsals, our class made a much-needed trip around the nature trail. "Look, Mrs. Kissner! A new trail!" Natalie exclaimed. She was right—the custodian had mowed us a new trail, right through the meadow. We meandered along, taking in the new perspective of the forest, wetland, and creek.

Hunter appeared at my side. "Mrs. Kissner, are there different kinds of grass?"

I looked at what he held. In one hand, there was a long strand of grass with thin, narrow seeds; in the other, a strand of grass that looked fairly similar but had wider, thicker seeds. In the meadow, surrounded by almost an acre of tall stalks, I probably would not have seen the difference.

"There are different kinds of grass," I said. "Wow! It looks like you found some."

"Yeah," he said. "And if you pull on the pods of this one, there are seeds inside. Look." He demonstrated.

"Neat," I agreed.

"Do you know what kind they are?" he asked. I shook my head no. He shrugged and continued. "It doesn't matter. I'm going to find more." Over the course of the next twenty minutes, he also found a low-growing, reddish form of grass, a tall stalk that looked like wheat, and a clump of cattails.

"There's a lot of stuff out here, Mrs. Kissner," he said. "I'm glad we came today."

Looking at him, his arms laden with drooping treasures, I agreed. I was glad we had come also. Not only had we explored a new trail, but I had seen the results of teaching kids to look for details. For Hunter, suddenly the world was full of hawks.

What to Remember: Helping Students to Pay Attention to Details

- Children often remember generalizations they have made but forget the details they used to form those generalizations.

- Taking students outdoors can help them to notice patterns, small changes, and little details.

- Outdoor activities to build an awareness of details should be well structured.

- "Paying attention" requires the mental currency of energy.

- As students try to focus on details, they must be able to filter out distractors from the environment.

- Playing the Distraction Game can help students understand how they can control the attention process.

ASSESSING HOW STUDENTS USE DETAILS

3

Every year, I get a fresh crop of students—students who come to me with a unique range of needs and abilities. I need to hit the ground running and get started with instruction as soon as I can. But what is the best way to learn about my students?

Each August brings me a new stack of folders for students, filling my filing cabinet. I have DRA (Developmental Reading Assessment) scores, DWA (Developing Writers Assessment) scores, and PSSA (Pennsylvania System of School Assessment) scores, all printed out in charts and graphs and standardized and created by people who theoretically know what they are doing. But although these numbers can get me headed in a certain direction, I'm still lost in the dark forest that separates where students are—what they are actually doing and thinking—from where I want them to be.

I can look at the PSSA score and say, "Wow, this student really needs to work on critically interpreting text." But how do I get the child to improve? Tell him to go and practice interpreting? No, I need to figure out what the little pieces of "critically interpreting text" can be, see what the child can and cannot do, and work from there.

To help me find my way, I have developed focused, simple, classroom-based assessments. Most of these assessments started out informally, as something I used on Tuesday to help me plan guided reading groups for Thursday. Over the years, I refined them and noticed what certain types of responses in September meant for a student's comprehension in May. From such simple beginnings, these assessments have become enormously useful as I plan to help students make sense of details. They are little lights that brightly illuminate my next few steps. They show me the way to travel, a little bit at a time.

Using Details to Build Visual Images from a Passage

I need to find out early in the year who is visualizing and who is not. With the rise of more strategies-based instruction, most students can now parrot back to me what visualizing means and how to use it. But I'm still curious to see how they put the strategy into practice.

When I handed out the Visualizing Assessment form (Figure 3–1) in the first week of school, students attacked the task with relish. "I'm not

Visualizing Assessment

Directions: Read the paragraph below. In the box, draw a picture of the scene it describes.

There was a spooky house on Erin's street. It was made out of brick and seemed to tower over everything else. The crumbling chimney looked as if it was about to fall on the sagging roof. Shutters hung by their hinges next to the second-floor windows, which had tattered curtains hanging in them. The porch looked like it would fall down at any moment. Erin stared at the weedy, overgrown walkway and the bushes that clustered around the front door. She couldn't imagine being brave enough to walk inside. But there was one thing that seemed out of place. The doorbell was bright and shiny, as if it were brand-new.

Figure 3–1.

interested in your drawing ability as much as I am interested in seeing how you think about the details from the text," I told the students. However, many students still did haul out their brand-new colored pencils or marker sets to faithfully record the details from the passage.

I designed the paragraph for the assessment carefully. I wanted to use something that would have some appeal to students. Haunted houses and spooky places are big favorites for intermediate students, and they are not difficult to draw. Also, I wanted the topic to tap into the students' prior knowledge to see how they would use what they already know about the topic to create a mental image. Finally, I needed one detail that stood out from the rest—the bright and shiny doorbell. I placed that one detail at the end of the passage and introduced it with a sentence to make it stand out: "But there was one thing that seemed out of place."

This assessment could easily be customized for different groups of students. To add to the challenge, try inserting a critical detail without a sentence of introduction. Many mysteries and thrillers bury details in this way, so a visualizing assessment like this would be useful to give before reading novels in these genres. A topic that is not immediately appealing would also increase the difficulty of the task and help the teacher see which students can maintain their focus in a less than interesting reading selection. Even more challenging would be a selection in which the main idea is implicit rather than clearly stated.

To find out about the visualizing processes of younger students, you may want to try a series of sentences that progress from simple to more complex. "The red race car zoomed up the hill" is easier to visualize than "The murky river snaked through the busy town." For students in third grade and below, reading sentences aloud and having kids draw what they envision can enable you to see whether poor performance on the task stems from a weak ability to visualize or poor decoding skills.

What information can you learn from this? Using the Visualizing Assessment Scoring Tool (Figure 3–2), I can easily find out which students are able to pull on their prior knowledge to build a visual image. I can also see which students pay attention to a critical detail in the text.

Let's look at several student responses to the Visualizing Assessment form and examine the drawings in relation to the scoring tool.

Bria is a lively, creative student who loves to read. In Figure 3–3, notice the detail that she included in her drawing. Her picture definitely represented the main idea of the passage, showing a ramshackle house next to one that is neat and tidy. She included many details that were not specifically mentioned in the text but were consistent with the details provided—for instance, a sidewalk and road leading down the street. Notice how she used her prior knowledge to depict the scene. Bria obviously knew what a chimney was and where it should go; she could picture the shutters hanging from their hinges; and she understood what the word *overgrown* means. The spooky house was not the only item pictured but

---

Visualizing Assessment Scoring Tool

Student name _____ Date _____

Check the box that best describes the student's response.

	Student represents the main idea of the passage.
	Drawing shows evidence of prior knowledge use (additional details that are consistent with the text, elaboration, etc.).
	Relationships between objects are shown.
	Critical or unexpected detail is present.

FIGURE 3–2.

was placed along the street with another house, showing that she can place items in relationship to one another. It's interesting that she put the tattered curtains on the first-floor windows instead of the second floor. Is this a major problem? Because the tattered curtains detail was buried in a sentence with other facts, a proficient reader could determine that it was not a key detail. If the curtains in the second floor were tattered, it was quite reasonable to guess that the first-floor curtains would be tattered as well. Finally, Bria showed the key detail, the doorbell, clearly next to the door. It's obvious that Bria spent time and energy visualizing what she read.

Does this mean that Bria should be finished with visualizing? Absolutely not! As you will read in Chapter 7, visualizing continues to be an important skill for readers of all skill levels. Bria has shown that she can visualize a scene from one moment in time. It will be interesting to see how she conceptualizes details as a story unfolds. Can she track visual details through time and space? How does she deal with images that contradict her prior knowledge?

Brendan gave me his picture with a rueful smile. "I'm not much of an artist," he said.

"That's not a problem," I assured him. Indeed, his picture (Figure 3–4) showed me many important features about his visualizing. I would rate Brendan's picture as doing a fair job of depicting the main idea of the

FIGURE 3–3. Bria's visualizing picture response

FIGURE 3–4. Brendan's visualizing picture response

passage. There was a house that looked somewhat spooky. However, he missed some other big ideas, including the rest of the neighborhood. Brendan did show evidence of prior knowledge use. His inclusion of a crescent moon was interesting. Such a moon does appear in many spooky pictures, it's true. But is there anything in the passage that leads the reader to conclude that the scene takes place at night? It could be that Brendan relied on his prior knowledge too much, substituting ideas from his brain for ideas that were stated in the passage. The relationships between items were not clearly shown. Notice that there were no second-story windows, no crumbling porch, no other houses. Did this mean that Brendan did not notice these details, or was he unable to draw them? It's hard to be sure. But he did show the critical detail and even added lines around it to show how bright and shiny it was.

As I learned throughout the school year, Brendan loved details. In fact, sometimes he got so caught up in the details of a piece that he missed main ideas or failed to see how details connect. But he learned how to notice the details that turn out to be important.

When compared to the other two, Samantha's drawing (Figure 3–5) looked quite different. I was surprised when I first looked at it. Samantha is a petite, quiet girl, always neat in her appearance and schoolwork. She gives no outward sign that she is struggling. However, her picture told a different story. It was difficult to see the main idea of the passage. Although there was some evidence of prior knowledge use, she didn't show many of the hallmarks of a haunted house. There were some relationships among the items in the passage, including the second-story shutters, but other details were missing altogether. What about the critical detail? It was

FIGURE 3–5. Samantha's visualizing picture response

hard to tell if the item she drew was a doorknob or a doorbell, and it certainly did not stand out in the drawing.

I think that Samantha, as a student, is characteristic of many of our struggling readers. She knows how to play the game of school and produce a product that teachers will accept. But there are gaps in her strategy use, including visualizing. Samantha's large-scale assessments show that she is just barely keeping at grade level. As text becomes more complex and demands more use of prior knowledge and critical details, she could easily fall behind.

As you can see, a simple assessment can give me some useful information about how students visualize. Because this is easy enough to give to the whole class and simple to score, I don't have to wait weeks to start worthwhile, targeted instruction.

But visualizing is not the only way that students can use details. Another important use of details is to find and use the critical details in a passage.

Finding and Using Critical Details in a Passage

One afternoon, I was talking with Matthew about the popular fantasy story *The Merchant of Death* from the Pendragon series (MacHale 2006). I noticed that his reading log didn't contain any character names.

"What is this boy called? He seems important," I said to Matthew.

"I forget his name," Matthew said, shrugging.

"That's probably something important to remember," I told him. This was an understatement! "Character names are important."

"He hasn't been in any chapters lately," Matthew replied. "I don't think he's in the story anymore."

I frowned. From reading many fantasies, I knew that characters rarely just disappear from a book. The "boy" that Matthew was talking about would probably return later and play an important role. Many students fail to remember important pieces of information as they read. When they ignore key details, they don't make an important kind of inference called a *text-based inference*.

Text-based inferences are the inferences that depend on a critical fact from the text. After reading about the importance of text-based inferences, I decided to create an assessment to see how students could remember and use rules and critical details. I realized that this assessment could also give me some insight into how students were developing their written responses to reading.

Using a neat detail that I remembered from catching insects with students, I wrote the story "Insect Hunt" and the accompanying question (see Figure 3–6). This short story has several features. Most important, the story challenges students to make an inference based on the information that is given. The reader needs to combine the "rule" that crickets have long antennae with the "critical fact" that the insect that Laura and

Insect Hunt

Laura's class was getting ready for a bug hunt. First, they read about the kinds of insects they might find. Laura worked with her group to browse through a pile of books about different insects.

"Look," said Kelsey, showing Laura a book about grasshoppers. "In this book, it says that grasshoppers don't have wings until the very last time they molt, or shed their skin."

"Wow," said Laura. "I'm reading about crickets. Did you know that some crickets can be green?"

"Hm," Kelsey said. She examined the picture in Laura's book. "If some crickets are green, and some grasshoppers are green, how can you tell the difference?"

Laura knew the answer. "It says here to look at the antennae," she replied. "Crickets have long antennae. Grasshoppers have short ones."

Laura and Kelsey kept looking at the books until their teacher said that it was time to go. They went and gathered the equipment for the insect hunt. There were magnifying glasses, plastic cups for collecting insects, special sweep nets, clipboards and paper, and the insect field guides.

"Today is a warm day," Mrs. Heath said as the class walked out to the meadow. "There should be plenty of insects around. Oops—I almost stepped on one!"

Laura laughed. Wherever she placed her foot, a cloud of insects jumped away. "I never knew there were so many bugs out here!" she said to Kelsey.

"We don't even need the nets," Kelsey agreed. Kneeling, she gently tried to catch an insect. It jumped out of her hands.

"Let me get it," Laura said. She reached for a plastic cup and tried to put it over the insect. After a few tries, she managed to trap the little bug inside. "There you are," she said, covering the top of the cup with her hand.

"Make sure it can breathe," Kelsey said. She peered at the insect. "Do you mind holding it while I draw the picture?"

Laura held the paper cup so that Kelsey could see it. "Hm," Kelsey said. "It's got six legs, and it's kind of green."

"It has wings," Laura said.

"You're right," said Kelsey. "And look at how long its antennae are!"

Did Laura and Kelsey find a grasshopper or a cricket? Support your answer with specific details from the text.

_____

_____

_____

_____

Figure 3–6.

Kelsey found had long antennae to infer that Laura and Kelsey found a cricket. To add to the challenge, I also presented some of the information in dialogue, because I have noticed that many students tend to skip over dialogue as unimportant.

Scoring Insect Hunt is somewhat more complex than scoring the Visualizing Assessment. There are two different important elements to look for. First, I look to see if students made the correct inference. Did they realize that Laura and Kelsey found a cricket, because it has long antennae? When students report that the insect is a grasshopper, I know that these students are having trouble. They may rely too much on their own background knowledge instead of paying attention to the details in the text.

I created the Insect Hunt Scoring Tool (Figure 3–7) to help me score this assessment, which I use at the start of the year. Student responses are always interesting!

Bridget, a quiet student with a strong work ethic, produced one of the stronger responses (Figure 3–8). Not only did she make a correct inference, but she supported this with both the rule (the book said that crickets have longer antennae) and the critical fact (Kelsey said how long the antennaes were). Her response could still use some development and some more connecting words. However, it showed that she was able to make text-based inferences.

Crystal's response (Figure 3–9) is slightly different from Bridget's. Although it looked longer, it actually was less developed. Crystal just gave the rule that crickets have longer antennae. She failed to show the connection between the rule and the task at hand. Of the twenty-three students in my class, seventeen responded with either the rule only or the critical fact only. This just led to more questions about their processing. Were some students just lazy and unwilling to write the extra sentence or two? Did they have the metacognitive ability to trace their mental processes to figure out how they made their inference? Were they having trouble keeping all of the relevant information in their working memories? I suspected that there many reasons behind the poorly developed answers. In Chapter 5, I explain some of the instructional strategies I used to work with students to improve their understanding of the inference process.

There were four students in my class who failed to make the correct inference. Two of their answers were especially fascinating. Mara showed an overreliance on prior knowledge and wrote that the girls had found a grasshopper, because crickets are black. The rule in the text was not strong enough to overcome what Mara assumed she already knew. Matt produced an equally interesting response, stating that the insect was a grasshopper because it had wings, and grasshoppers have wings after the last time they molt. Both of these responses showed me some of the strategies that these students were using and shed light on how I could help them improve.

Insect Hunt Scoring Tool

Student name _____ Date _____

- **Target inference:** Laura and Kelsey found a cricket.
- **Rule:** Crickets have long antennae.
- **Critical fact:** The insect that Laura and Kelsey found had long antennae.

Check the box that best describes the student's response.

	Correct inference, supported by both rule and critical fact
	Correct inference, supported by rule
	Correct inference, supported by critical fact
	Correct inference, incorrect or no support
	No inference, correct information from text
	Incorrect inference, supported by faulty prior knowledge
	Response does not answer question

If assistance was provided, please check any appropriate boxes.

	Passage read aloud to student
	Support provided in finding critical fact
	Support provided in finding rule
	Question clarified

FIGURE 3–7.

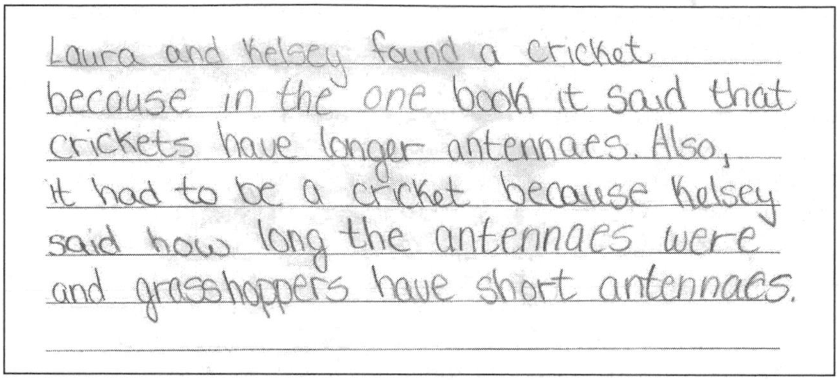
Laura and Kelsey found a cricket
because in the one book it said that
crickets have longer antennaes. Also,
it had to be a cricket because Kelsey
said how long the antennaes were
and grasshoppers have short antennaes.

FIGURE 3–8. Bridget's Insect Hunt response

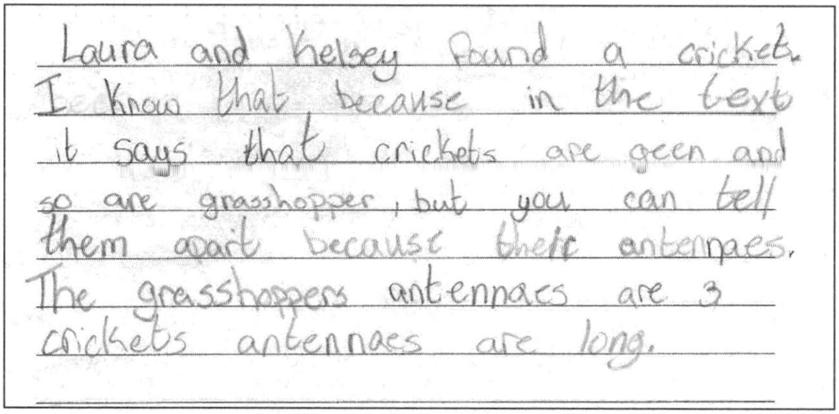
Laura and Kelsey found a cricket.
I Know that because in the text
it says that crickets are geen and
so are grasshopper, but you can tell
them apart because their antennaes.
The grasshoppers antennaes are 3
crickets antennaes are long.

FIGURE 3–9. Crystal's Insect Hunt response

Supporting an Inference with Details

Text-based inferences are not the only kind of inference. Sometimes a reader must use prior knowledge to make an inference. In this case, the "rule" to make the inference is drawn from the reader's own memory (Bowyer-Crane and Snowling 2005). Consider the sentence "Julia, sweating in the hot sun, reached for her cup." From prior knowledge about cups and the hot sun, you will probably infer that the cup contained a cold drink. Of course, the more general knowledge and background experiences a reader possesses, the easier knowledge-based inferences become.

I knew that one assessment could not give me a perfect view of my students' skill with knowledge-based inferences. What could I create that would give me the most information, especially information relevant to our state tests? I decided to do a typical character traits kind of question. Many reading tasks ask students to assign traits to characters based on their actions and words. This requires the reader to make a knowledge-based inference. In order to call a character greedy, for instance, the reader has to draw from prior knowledge about what the word *greedy* means and compare that to the character's actions in the story.

I wrote "Nature Walk" (Figure 3–10) as a way to assess students' ability to generate and support knowledge-based inferences. I have learned that writing my own stories to share in the classroom is a certain way to get my students motivated. When I introduced "Nature Walk," I told students, "I wrote this story a few months ago, but I couldn't think of a way to end it. One night an ending just came to me. I'd like you to read it and answer the question, but I'd also like you to tell me if the ending works for you. Do you think this story has potential?" Even a simple assessment activity can engage the children in real conversation. (The consensus was that they liked the story, but wanted to know more about Ben. Several demanded a sequel.) If you want to encourage this kind of conversation in your classroom, try writing your own story for an assessment task. When students see you taking risks, the entire classroom environment changes to a place where academic risks are challenged and encouraged.

Once students had taken the assessment (Figure 3–11), I needed to find a way to make sense of their results. On our state assessment, a task-specific scoring guide is used, with students getting scores ranging from 0 to 3. I decided to dispense with the number score and simply write descriptors for the different responses that I saw from students.

Students never fail to surprise me, and Abigail's response (Figure 3–12) was no exception. Notice that she did not list a specific trait, but instead used the phrase "not afraid to go his own way" to describe Ben. Because the question asked her to use a word or phrase to describe Ben, this was acceptable. She supported her response with a detail from the text, the fact that Ben kept looking at an animal despite being told by the teacher to stick with the group. Additional support here, in the form of some more specific evidence, would have strengthened her response. However, this kind of support is quite difficult for students, as you will see in Chapter 13, which focuses on helping students to write these kinds of short-answer responses.

Abigail's response had a sentence left over from a time when all students were expected to show a personal connection to the text in every response, even when the question did not explicitly cue them to do so. The sentence "I think if I was Ben I would have done the same ezact thing" was not really needed in this task.

Bridget's response (Figure 3–13) looked like it had everything it needed. She used two specific trait words to describe Ben—*confident* and *curious*. She also gave a detail for each to explain why the traits fit Ben. Notice, though, that there was no connection between the traits and the supports. "Ben is confident when he told everyone about the other animals,"

Nature Walk

Ben looked around at the woods. He was excited to go on a nature walk with his class.

"What do you think we will see today?" asked the naturalist, Mr. Mark.

Students raised their hands. "Owls!" "Bats!" "Rabbits!" "Lions!" "Hawks!" "Snakes!"

Mr. Mark laughed and raised his hand. This was the signal for students to be quiet. "Well, we have to be realistic. That means we need to think about what can really happen. Even though we want to see all of those animals, we probably won't."

Ben spoke up. "And lions don't even live around here." His teacher, across the circle, put her finger to her lips. She wanted Ben to be quiet.

"We won't see any animals?" Erik asked.

"Probably not," said Mr. Mark. "But I have lots of other neat things to show you. As you walk, I want you to pay attention to the things that I show you. I am the nature expert, and I have lots to share with you. Let's go."

They set off into the forest. Ben noticed that there were different kinds of trees. Some were evergreen trees, with sharp green needles. Some were oak trees, dropping acorns into the trail. And some were maple trees, with yellow leaves.

"Ah, look at this!" Mr. Mark exclaimed. The class stopped. He was pointing to some litter. "This is something that shouldn't be in the forest."

He went on to tell the class about all of the problems that litter causes.

Ben tried to listen politely, but he couldn't see very well. And he knew about litter. Instead, he walked a few feet away from the group, back down the trail. He was looking up into the trees. And there, on a high branch, he spotted something amazing.

There was a bird on a branch. It was light brown and perfectly still. An owl!

He looked to where his class was learning about litter. They had already started moving up the trail. His teacher was waiting for him. "Come on, Ben. You need to stay with the group."

"But I saw"—

"Shh. We need to catch up with the rest of the class."

Ben followed his teacher. He couldn't believe that he had actually seen an owl! During the daytime!

They walked over rocks. They walked up a hill and down a steep bank. Then the class stopped again. "Look at this! It's really cool!" said Mr. Mark. He called the class over. "See the moss that's growing here? Feel how soft it is."

Ben felt the moss. He liked how it was cool and green. He went a few steps away and felt a different kind of moss that grew on a large white rock. As he leaned down to look more closely, he realized that there were two eyes looking back at him. A toad!

He looked back at the class. They were still learning about moss. "Look what I found!" he called.

FIGURE 3–10.

Nature Walk *(continued)*

"We need to get moving," said Mr. Mark. "We have many more things to see."

"But I saw"—

"Ben," said his teacher. "You need to do a better job."

Ben glanced back at the toad as he followed his class. He had seen an owl and a toad. This trip was turning out to be great.

When the class stopped again, Mr. Mark showed them a mushroom. Ben saw a tiny caterpillar inching its way across a tree trunk. After they walked over a wooden bridge and up a hill, the class looked at another piece of litter. Ben saw a kingfisher swooping down over the creek.

"And here," said Mr. Mark, "is a very exciting place. It is called a bird blind. We can stand behind the wooden structure and look at birds. They won't see us, but we will see them."

The class gathered in the bird blind and clustered around the tiny windows. There wasn't enough room for Ben, so he looked at the wooden frame instead. Then he looked closer. Another caterpillar was crawling across, but one that was completely different from the other one that he had seen. He wondered if he should tell the rest of his class, and then decided not to.

When the class looked at a gray rock, Ben saw deer tracks in the mud. While the class studied a tree that had been struck by lightning, Ben saw a high cloud make a rainbow in the sky.

Finally the class reached the nature center. "Let's make a list of what we saw," said Mr. Mark. "We'll go around the circle so everyone has a turn."

When it was Ben's turn, he said, "I saw an owl, a toad, a caterpillar, a kingfisher, and deer tracks," Ben said. "Oh, and some neat clouds that made a rainbow."

The other students were staring at him. Mr. Mark put down the chalk. "Really?" he asked, sounding interested. Then he laughed. "Well, everyone," he said. "If your teacher says it's okay, I think we should go back on the nature trail. And this time, we should let the real expert lead us. Okay, Ben?"

Ben grinned. His teacher was looking at him in astonishment. "Okay," Ben said. "Let's go."

Short-Answer Response Question

What words or phrases could you use to describe Ben? Use specific details from the text to support your response.

_____

_____

_____

_____

_____

FIGURE 3–10. *continued*

Nature Walk Scoring Tool

Student name _____ Date _____

- **Target inference:** A word or phrase to describe Ben
- **Rule:** Specific detail or event from the story
- **Connection:** Shows how the support proves the word or phrase

Check the box that best describes the student's response.

	Inference includes a specific trait, specific support, and a clear connection between the support and the trait.
	Inference includes a specific trait, an attempt at support, and an attempt at a connection between the support and the trait.
	Inference includes a specific trait and some support.
	Inference includes an attempt at a trait, with scanty or implicit support.
	Inference includes a trait only, no support.
	No inference, correct information from text.
	Incorrect inference, supported by faulty prior knowledge.
	Response does not answer question.

If assistance was provided, please check any appropriate boxes.

	Passage read aloud to student
	Support provided in finding critical fact
	Support provided in finding rule
	Question clarified

FIGURE 3–11.

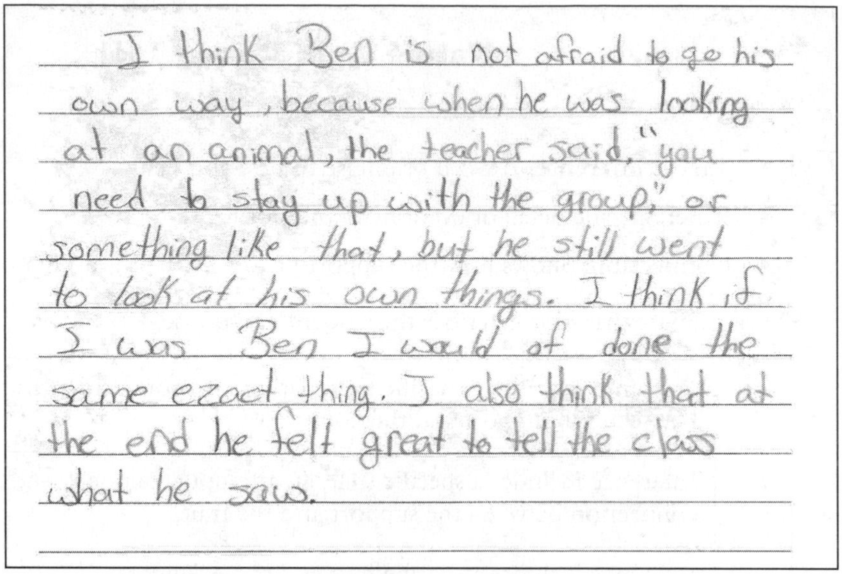

> I think Ben is not afraid to go his own way, because when he was looking at an animal, the teacher said, "you need to stay up with the group," or something like that, but he still went to look at his own things. I think, if I was Ben I would of done the same ezact thing. I also think that at the end he felt great to tell the class what he saw.

FIGURE 3–12. Abigail's Nature Walk response

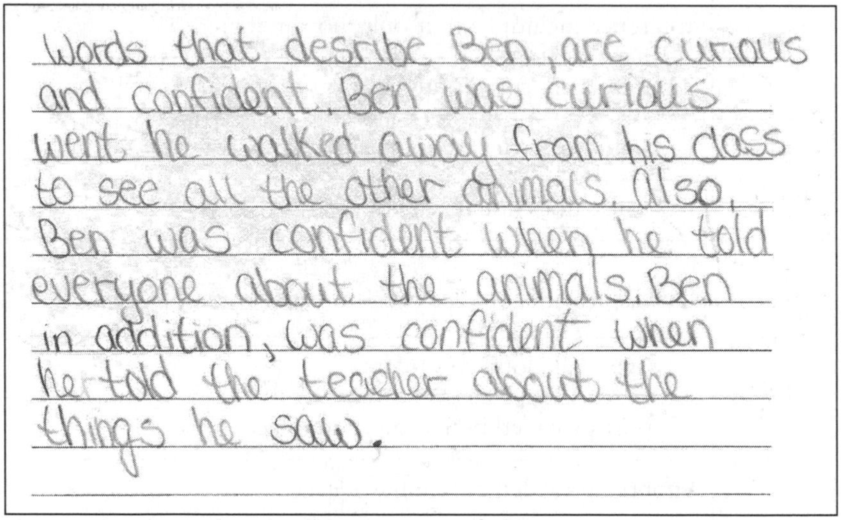

> Words that desribe Ben, are curious and confident. Ben was curious went he walked away from his class to see all the other animals. Also, Ben was confident when he told everyone about the animals. Ben in addition, was confident when he told the teacher about the things he saw.

FIGURE 3–13. Bridget's Nature Walk response

Bridget wrote, and yet she did not explain why this action would demonstrate that someone is confident. In other words, Bridget asked the person reading her response to make an inference!

But why does it really matter? I can tell that Bridget read and understood the story. She used decent details to support her trait. Isn't it just splitting hairs to say, "Well, it could be better?" I used to think so. However, we do students like Bridget a disservice if we just nod and praise their pretty good work. Bridget assumed that her reader uses the same definition of *confident* as she did. This is a safe assumption for sixth grade. As Bridget progresses in her academic life, though, she will find herself in situations in which she and her readers do not share such an intimate context. She will have to explain her reasoning more carefully if she is to make herself clear, and she will have to be able to trace back through her own thought processes to figure out how she came to her conclusions. Once Bridget masters this, she will have no limits.

Let me tell you a little bit about Ian. He worked for weeks to keep hourly weather data from our school's weather station. He cultivated at least twelve different plants on the plant table, taking care of them and guarding them from the attention of other students. He started a newspaper, tried to learn German, and created a terrarium in the classroom. In other words, Ian is pretty crazy about the details. But you wouldn't be able to tell from reading his response!

Ian's response (Figure 3–14) was pretty typical of what sixth-grade boys create. He gave an answer, supported it with the barest of details, and turned it in. Done and done. He includes some great traits but did not pull the specific details he needed to support them or explain how the support linked back to the trait. Why do boys respond this way so often? Is it because they have trouble pulling the specific support, or do they just not like to write? I'm not sure.

Conclusion

Helping students create knowledge-based inferences is a process that spans the school year. The more I learn about my students, the more questions I have. The assessment process has shown me that each student brings a fascinating set of experiences, strategies, and anomalies to the task of reading. Through the assessments detailed in this chapter, I start to solve the puzzle of who my students are and how to teach them.

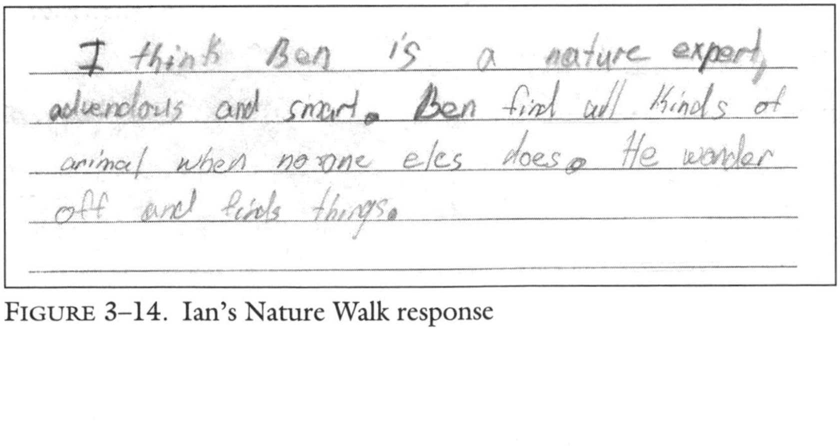

FIGURE 3–14. Ian's Nature Walk response

As I learned about how students process details, I encountered one more burning question. What are the processes that readers use to recognize and take note of details in text? Why is it that some readers seem to process text in a different way than others? My search for the answers was about to lead me back to some pretty interesting theories.

What to Remember About Classroom Assessments

- Simple classroom assessments can give a teacher strong information about what students can and can't do.

- The visualizing assessment yields information about how students make mental pictures.

- A story like "Insect Hunt" can be used to assess whether students are making text-based inferences.

- A story like "Nature Walk" can be used to see how students are using their prior knowledge to make text-based inferences.

HOW READERS
PROCESS DETAILS

4

Finding out how my students interact with details in text has only led me to more questions. How can I account for the difference between how students use details in real life and how they process details in reading? What is really going on in students' minds as they read text and consider the details?

To answer these questions, I needed to do some research.

Three Levels of Text Processing: A Brief Explanation

Combing through the journals, I discovered a whole host of researchers who are working on what they describe as three levels of text representation. What follows is a very brief primer on these three levels and what they mean, and then a description of how the three levels of text processing might look in the classroom.

In 1983, Walter Kintsch and Teun van Dijk proposed the idea that a text is represented in the memory of the reader at three different levels: the surface level, the textbase, and the situation model (van Dijk and Kintsch 1983).

The first level, or *surface level*, is where the reader remembers exact words and punctuation. In general, a reader only remembers the most recent sentence at the surface level. Representation at the surface level is quick and fleeting, and requires only the shallowest of processing (Graesser, Millis, and Zwaan 1997). If you have ever read the words of a text without understanding the sentences and ideas, you've experienced reading at just the surface level.

As a reader links one idea to the next, the *textbase* is formed. This is a literal understanding of the main ideas of a text, combining the individual words into a series of coherent propositions. At the textbase level, the reader considers how individual words connect, how they form ideas, and how one sentence relates to another. Perhaps you have looked up from a text and tried to restate the main ideas. As you consider how the ideas fit together, you have built a textbase.

The third level of text processing, the *situation model*, is where interesting thinking takes place. This is where the reader actively connects new information to old, makes predictions, and dialogues with the text. New information is synthesized into existing schema. Have you ever found yourself looking up from a text when you encountered an idea or thought that surprised you? Have you ever felt that you were so deeply engrossed in the text that you were actually experiencing the main character's problems? These are examples of the situation model at work. The situation model is always changing, as ideas from the text interact with the readers' background and experiences.

For skilled readers, it is easy to navigate quickly through the three levels of text processing to come to a well-developed understanding of a selection. For our students, though, it can be more difficult. Some students do not move past the surface level to create a well-developed textbase or a literal understanding of the text. These readers equate sounding out the words with reading skill. Other readers get to the literal understanding of the text, but don't activate their prior knowledge to make connections or develop inferences. The three levels of text processing have enormous implications for the classroom teacher.

Three Levels of Text Processing in the Classroom

As I learned about the three levels of processing, I began to look for evidence of how my students were moving through the surface model, textbase, and situation model. I hoped to hear comments in my guided reading groups, or students' own literature discussion groups, that would help me determine this. But one of my first experiences turned out to be during a practice assessment for our state standardized tests.

I had gotten the article, a short piece about chocolate, from the state's bank of public release items. It was at the fifth-grade level, which would work for most of my students. Best of all, it was about the history of chocolate—a topic that I knew would be intrinsically motivating for my students.

As soon as I handed out the papers, however, the students revealed that they already had a surface level memory of the text. "This looks familiar," Arturo said.

"I think this was on the PSSA last year," Bria said. Scattered comments from around the room confirmed that this text had not been written simply as a task to put on the website to show teachers what to expect. It had been on the actual fifth-grade test.

So, as usual, I had to make a quick decision. Keep the test or scrap it? "Sometimes it's useful to read a text more than one time," I told the class. "And I've developed some more questions to go along with it. Read it again and see what new things you learn. I'll be interested to hear about your thinking."

The students agreed. "You know, even though this was on the test, I don't really remember what it was talking about," Arturo said, more to himself than to me. This is typical of surface-level processing. A reader might remember what a text looks like, or remember a few key words, but does not recall main ideas or link new information to prior knowledge.

After a few moments, Thomas called me over. I knelt by his desk, expecting a question.

"This is all about cocoa and how they once used it as money," he said. "I'm glad we're reading it again. It says in here that the first use of chocolate was as a drink, but not like hot chocolate."

I waited a moment, but he seemed to go back to his reading. "Do you have a question?" I finally asked.

"No," he said breezily. "I just wanted to tell you that."

"Oh," I answered. "Thank you."

By identifying a topic of the text and some key pieces of information, Thomas showed that he was well on his way to developing a textbase. I looked up to see that Bria had her hand raised on the other side of the room. I knelt down beside her.

"Can you make healthier chocolate?" she asked.

I was startled by the question. When students beckoned me to come over during reading tests, they usually wanted clarification on a question or a set of directions. This question was quite unusual. "Do you mean, can I personally make healthier chocolate right now, or can healthier chocolate be made?" I cautiously asked Bria.

"Can healthier chocolate be made?" she mused. "It says here that the cocoa butter doesn't mix with water, and it has to be mixed with fat. But in phys ed we learned that fat isn't healthy. So could we mix the cocoa butter with something else?"

As Bria thought through the process of creating healthier chocolate, she was giving me a glimpse into her situation model. She was combining information from the text with her own prior knowledge to generate new questions and understandings. Instead of feeling disengaged from a routine repeated reading, she was actively engaged with the selection. (About a week later, she came to me with a recipe that she had written, replacing some of the fat in chocolate with tomato juice.)

In one short classroom activity, I was able to notice how students processed text at three levels. By remembering that they had read the article before, they showed me that they had created a surface-level representation. Thomas built a textbase when he put ideas from the text into his own words. And Bria's thinking about how the process of making chocolate related to what she had learned in physical education class showed me that she was processing the text at the level of the situation model. What's more, I was beginning to understand how text details relate to all three levels of text processing.

The Three Levels of Text Processing and Details
How do details fit in with these three levels of text processing? If students are just developing a surface-level understanding of a text, they probably don't see the details. Although the students in my class knew that they had read the article about chocolate before, they couldn't remember any

of the facts from the text. None of them remembered that chocolate had once been used as currency or that chocolate contains important antioxidants. These details simply do not register at the surface level.

As students develop a textbase, the details come into play. Remember, the textbase is where a literal representation of the text is formed in the reader's mind, proposition by proposition. Often, the details help to illustrate a point or make it more understandable. Sometimes a detail is needed for a student to generate an inference that links ideas or events.

Details are especially important at the level of the situation model. It is often a detail that will trigger a memory of prior knowledge. For Bria, reading about the way that cocoa butter works spurred her to remember information from phys ed class. In fiction, a detail can often evoke vivid images and memories that help us to make sense of a text—for instance, a detail about a long row of lockers and the gleam of freshly waxed floors might make a reader remember the first day of high school and make predictive inferences about what might happen next in the story. And sometimes a seductive detail is so interesting and juicy that it can pull a reader away from the meaning of a text altogether, leading to an impaired situation model and flawed comprehension.

As I help students improve their understanding of the text they read, I find it useful to think about how they are processing that text. When students cannot retell what they have read, I know that they need to work on generating a coherent textbase. And when they fail to make inferences, visualizations, or generalizations, I know that I need to guide them toward creating a situation model.

Conclusion

When readers encounter a text, they represent that text in their minds at three different levels: the surface level, the textbase, and the situation model. Although the surface-level representation is quite brief, the textbase and the situation model can be remembered over a long period of time. The textbase is the literal understanding of a text. When a reader combines new information from the text with prior knowledge, the situation model is created.

An understanding of text processing is necessary for understanding how some of the detail-related strategies work. In the next chapters, we'll examine how details are important for a number of key reading strategies. We'll also see how details can help students move beyond the shallow processing of the surface level and into the important levels of the textbase and situation model.

What to Remember About Text Processing

- Readers process text at three levels: the surface level, the textbase, and the situation model.

- The surface level is a brief, shallow processing of the surface features of the text.

- A reader creates a textbase by linking ideas together to form a literal understanding of the text.

- The situation model is the level at which new information interacts with the reader's prior knowledge.

5 TEXT-BASED INFERENCES

As we we rode the bus to a local camp for a field trip, Andrea pointed out the window at a corner piece of property, shrouded in dense woods. "See that place there?" she said. "Someone put a gorilla up in a tree and left it there."

I struggled to understand what she was saying. As the bus rumbled by, I caught a glimpse of white and gray fur. A gorilla? In a tree? What kind of people lived here?

"Yeah, I went bike riding there once," Arturo said. "There are lots of flamingos back in the woods. They really scared us at first, because it was all dark back there and we didn't know what they were."

Gorillas in a tree? Frightening flamingos? I knew that we lived in a rural area and that people kept some pretty exotic pets. There was a game park a few miles away, an elk farm somewhere in the hills, an emu farm, and llamas. I was worried for Arturo's safety. "Why were you riding your bike back there? Is that safe?"

He shrugged. "Oh yeah, sure." Seeing my puzzled expression, he added, "They're not real, you know. They're the plastic kind." He started laughing. "And it's just a stuffed gorilla up in the tree."

"Oh!" Suddenly I understood, and felt a rush of embarrassment at the crazy ideas I'd had. I laughed. "I was thinking, what kind of person would put a gorilla in a tree?" The students laughed too, enjoying a joke at my expense.

What had gone wrong in our conversation? Based on what Andrea said, I had started making inferences about the plot of land she had shown me. As I heard more information, it became more and more apparent that my inference didn't match the situation. I had drawn on the available details and my own prior knowledge to come to a conclusion that didn't match reality.

In conversation and in reading, we make inferences all the time. An inference is a logical guess based on available information and details from prior knowledge, previous points in the text, or experience. When readers share a context and are able to pull from similar background experiences, rich inferences can be made. Good readers enjoy the feeling of being pulled into a text, understanding the implications of a subtle gesture or a quiet comment. Inference making is at the heart of humor, especially when a joke leads the reader to make an inference that turns out to be false.

But when speakers or readers do not share a context, sometimes inferences are made incorrectly or not made at all. In the example above, I made an incorrect inference because I failed to realize that Andrea was referring to a stuffed gorilla. Andrea didn't think she needed to specify the kind of gorilla—a real gorilla in the woods of Adams County was completely outside the bounds of her context. I had seen unusual animals on some local farms, though, and I was willing to stretch the bounds of my context to allow for this new development.

To truly understand a paragraph, some researchers estimate that a reader will need to generate twelve to fifteen different inferences (Weaver and Kintsch 1991). Not all of these inferences are generated in the same way, however. There are many different kinds of inferences, with different processes used to create them. To understand how our struggling—and not so struggling—readers can improve at making inferences, it's important to consider how inferences are made.

Obviously, inferring is an important skill, and one that depends on understanding how to use the details of text. The next few chapters will look at how and why to teach inferring in the classroom. In this chapter, we will look at text-based inferences. In the next chapter, reader-based inferences will be discussed. As you will discover, knowing the difference between reader-based inferences and text-based inferences is useful in planning classroom instruction.

In Chapter 7, we will explore the idea of visualizing as a kind of extended inference.

Introducing Text-Based Inferences

Because inferences are so important for making meaning of text, I like to start working with inferring fairly early in the year. Teaching students about inferring can happen at many points during the day: whole-group instruction, read-aloud, and guided reading.

When I started teaching inferring in both fourth and sixth grades, I was relieved to find that many students already knew what an inference was. I was pleased to find that an equation in *The Comprehension Toolkit* succinctly states what an inference is: BK + TC = I. In other words, Background Knowledge plus Text Clues equals Inference (Harvey and Goudvis 2005). This equation, so easy to write and remember, has become my standard introduction to the world of inferring.

But what is the background knowledge of the text-based inference? Because these inferences are based mostly on clues in the text, they don't require the reader to pull on knowledge of baseball or camping or emotions. The background knowledge required is knowledge of how text works. To form a text-based inference, the reader needs to know what to expect from text and how to understand details such as pronouns, speaker tags, and quotation marks.

Beginning inference instruction with text-based inferences can help demystify the process of making inferences.

When an Inference Helps a Text Make Sense: Bridging Inferences

Bridging inferences, or cohesive inferences, are the inferences that readers make as they generate a coherent textbase. These are the inferences that keep a story together. As I looked at how my students read and processed text, I noticed difficulties with two kinds of bridging inferences: the inferences needed to understand multiple referents, or anaphors, and the inferences needed to understand who is speaking in dialogue. When students do not make these inferences, their comprehension suffers. I decided to focus on these inferences in guided reading.

Multiple Referents: Important Details

"I think the last story in the book looks interesting," Mark announced one day during guided reading, paging through the book *Surprises* (Goodman 1990). After several days of intensive instruction, I had offered this group the choice of the next story to read.

"Yeah, it has guns in it," Matt said. "That sounds cool."

I looked at the story, "Gold-Mounted Guns" somewhat dubiously. Originally written in 1925 (Buckley 1925), the story had been rewritten in *Surprises* (Goodman 1990) at an easier reading level. However, the story still placed some heavy demands on the reader, with a surprise ending that revealed a case of mistaken identity. But it was interesting and fast-paced and would emphasize some of the inference work we had been doing in class.

"That's what we'll read tomorrow, then," I agreed.

As I reread the story that night, I began to doubt my decision. How was I going to help this group of students understand the story? Although there are only two main characters, each one is referred to by at least four different names in the story. The entire ending hinges on an inference that one of the characters makes at the beginning. These are the kinds of details that can cause students to have comprehension problems. I knew that the students were excited to read the story, and that their motivation would help them cope with some of the challenges. Still, I was worried.

I began by making a list of all of the ways in which the author refers to each character. The main character, Will Arblaster, is also called "the boy," "newcomer," "the younger," and "the young man." I knew that my students would find the referents to both "boy" and "young man" to be problematic. I didn't want them thinking that there was another boy appearing in the story. Just telling the students the different referents would not generate the sort of active processing that I was hoping for. I needed to draw their attention to the details of the multiple referents in a concrete, visual way. So I got out my highlighters and started to work, marking the first page only of their copies with different colors to show the different characters. Here's how I introduced the lesson when we started the group.

"Sometimes, an author might talk about the same character in different ways. Does anyone have any ideas why an author might choose to do this?"

Tasha shrugged. "Because it might get boring to use the same words all the time?"

"Exactly," I said. "Think about how boring it would be if I repeated a character's name over and over. 'Tasha was so glad to come to reading. Tasha loved reading Tasha's book. Tasha was looking forward to reading a new story.'"

The students groaned at the repetition. Matt gave me a thumbs-down sign.

"Right, it sounds dull. So authors often use other words to add some variety. In the story we're going to read today, the author refers to the characters in several different ways. We need to use our inferring skills to figure out that these different names all refer to the same person. Keeping track of these different terms for characters will help us to keep track of what's going on."

I handed students a copy of the By Another Name worksheet (Figure 5–1). I had decided to create a generic page that could be used for any story instead of a page that was specific to our current reading. I read aloud the example, modeling how I thought through the different names for Kara. "Figuring out how the author uses different terms for different characters is a special kind of inference. You need to use your background knowledge of how a story works—for example, that *she* can refer to a girl. It's important because if I don't know who the author is talking about, then I can't really understand the story."

Next, I gave students the marked copy of the story. It was amusing to see how even sixth graders appreciated highlighted text. I explained to the students how I had highlighted the words that referred to one character in green and the words that referred to another character in blue.

I continued to explain how to do the rest of the By Another Name page. For each box, students collected the different words that the author used to refer to the characters. We worked on the first page together. "Here, I have highlighted *the boy* in green, to show that it refers to Will. How did I know that Will is the character who is being talked about here and that the author is not introducing another character?" We discussed the question and then moved on along the first page until I was satisfied that students understood how to pay attention to the

By Another Name

Authors often refer to the same character in different ways

All of these phrases refer to the same girl.

→ <u>Kara</u> turned a weedy patch into a beautiful garden.
→ <u>She</u> was not discouraged by the bugs or weeds. The
→ <u>young gardener</u> was very determined.

Directions: As you read your book or story, notice how the author often refers to the same character in different ways. Record all of these different ways in the chart below. You will need to add throughout the reading. Do not forget pronouns such as *he* and *she*.

Character 1	Character 2	Character 3
Name:	Name:	Name:
_____	_____	_____
Also known as:	Also known as:	Also known as:
_____	_____	_____
_____	_____	_____
_____	_____	_____
_____	_____	_____
_____	_____	_____

FIGURE 5–1.

© 2008 by Emily Kissner from *The Forest and the Trees*. Portsmouth, NH: Heinemann.

bridging inferences they needed to make. Then, students read the remainder of the story with a partner and continued on their own.

Despite my worries, the story worked particularly well for this activity, because the surprise ending reveals that the character believed to be the bandit Pecos Tommy is someone else entirely. The micro-level activity of resolving anaphors linked very well to the main idea of the text. As we discussed the story and the multiple referents the next day, I made sure students understood that the purpose of resolving the anaphors is to help a reader understand the story as a whole.

I want to urge a measure of caution for teachers. It might seem tempting to have students practice making these kinds of inferences over and over again, breaking down the story into individual sentences for practice. However, micro-level instruction is not totally effective in isolation. Several researchers worked to measure the effects of micro-level instruction, such as making these bridging inferences, versus macro-level instruction, such as identifying main ideas. After twelve training sessions, the students in the macro-level treatment outperformed the students who had undergone the micro-level instruction on tests of comprehension and summarizing (Gallini et al. 1993). This is not surprising—when students are instructed at the micro level, looking closely at individual sentences, they tend to continue to a micro-level focus. Interestingly, the study didn't measure the effects of instruction in both micro-level and macro-level concepts. My classroom experience has shown me that micro-level instruction can be highly effective when combined with teaching students to also look for main ideas. However, whenever I do micro-level work, such as studying multiple referents, I need to make sure that my students always return to the text as a whole.

Multiple referents are not the only kind of bridging inference. Much of the text that I read with students includes copious amounts of dialogue. And, as I noticed, understanding dialogue requires some serious inferring.

The Details of Dialogue

Hoping to liven up a discussion of a story we were reading, I quickly assigned students to read different parts. "Let's get started," I said. "Sara?"

Sara read to the end of the line. She came to a speaker tag, stopped, and didn't continue with the rest of the character's words. Two students came in together, trying to read the same line. The narrator looked at me in confusion. "Mrs. Kissner, who is supposed to be talking here?"

Instead of livening up the class, our attempt at reading the story aloud ended in disaster. Somehow, these sixth graders had never learned how to read dialogue. "I'll just read this part to you," I said, trying to get through the lesson quickly. I could tell that my students' problems with dialogue were more than I could fix in just a few moments.

Later, during independent reading time, I walked around the room to look in on what my students were reading. "How do you know who's talking?" I asked Julie, who was reading *PaperQuake: A Puzzle* by Kathryn Reiss (1998). Like most of Reiss' books, this one is dense with lengthy conversations, and much of the plot is revealed through dialogue.

"I mostly skip where people are talking," she told me. Then she laughed, looking abashed. "I guess I shouldn't have told you that."

Julie's statement was surprising to me. When I try to read a novel quickly, I usually do just the opposite: skip the paragraphs of exposition and read only the dialogue.

Next to her, James had a different answer. "Usually it tells you who's talking," he said, pointing to a speaker tag in the text.

I pointed to the next line, which was without a speaker tag. "What about when it doesn't say?" I asked.

He frowned. "That's the other guy talking now, right?" Scanning down through the next few lines of conversation, he said, "And then he goes on talking until it says *said* again, right?" James pointed to several lines of dialogue. He had missed the significance of new lines and indenting.

If students were skipping the dialogue or just guessing about who was talking, then what were they missing? In stories, dialogue carries some pretty important details. Not only can dialogue reveal information, but it also shows character and moves the story forward (Bauer 1992). The dialogue problem is an example of how inference can be layered upon inference. The bridging inference that allows students to know who is speaking leads to more elaborative inferences of character, plot, and theme. If students are not paying attention to the dialogue, they are missing multiple layers of meaning.

In my classroom, the problem of understanding dialogue is compounded by the expanding world of literature that students of this age enjoy. As texts become more complicated, more and more authors employ the lengthy conversation technique, going back and forth eight or ten times between speaker tags. This keeps the text interesting and fast-paced. It can also make it incomprehensible for readers who don't know how to make the appropriate bridging inferences.

Different Groups, Different Needs

At the time, I was getting ready to read *Mrs. Frisby and the Rats of NIMH* with the class (O'Brien 1986). Why were we all about to read the same text? With state tests approaching, I decided that all students needed to have exposure to grade-level text. They needed to experience the challenges that such text poses and learn coping strategies to help them succeed. So, even though all of the groups were about to read the same novel, I knew that I would have to alter my instruction for each group. My struggling readers would need much more structure and support to help them create a coherent textbase.

Mrs. Frisby has many episodes of conversation. Like other novels at this reading level, the author chose to keep the pace lively by occasionally eliminating speaker tags. As I looked at teaching the first section, I planned a variety of different lessons to help students make the necessary bridging inferences to figure out who was talking.

Whole-Class Lesson: Focusing on the Details of Dialogue. The lesson began with whole-group instruction. Before I started in guided reading groups, I wanted all students to have an introduction to the topic. I used the Who's Doing the Talking? worksheet (Figure 5–2) to give students an overview of why it is important to see which character is saying what. Besides giving students some basic rules for figuring out who is talking when, the handout includes an easy selection that provides an opportunity for students to put the rules into practice. As we discussed the handout together, I emphasized to students that I wanted them to point to the picture that corresponded to the character who was talking. The visual cue would help readers imagine which character was speaking.

High Level of Support. I met first with the students who needed a high level of support with the text. For these students, I made photocopies of the chapter we would be discussing. Even though students had their own books, I wanted pages that we could write on. Next, I highlighted Mrs. Frisby's lines pink and Mr. Ages' lines blue. I also found pictures of two mice and labeled one *Mrs. Frisby* and the other *Mr. Ages*. These were the names of the characters that were having the conversation in the text.

First, the students read along and used the pictures to point to the speakers as I read. After I read half of the page aloud, I was ready to hand over the control to the students. "Now it's time for your individual reading. As you continue to read, I want you to keep pointing to the character who is speaking. I'll be around to listen in as you read. After you are finished, I'd like you to try to explain what happened in this conversation in one or two sentences." Notice that I had students take the micro-level information of who was speaking back to a macro-level understanding of what the conversation was about.

This level of support worked well for the group. The highlighting provided the additional visual cue that they needed to understand the conversation, and the pictures helped them to match speaker to dialogue. In the days to come, I helped the students read conversations without the highlighting, gradually taking away the support as they improved.

Who's Doing the Talking?

How do we know who is talking?

- **Looking at speaker tags**—authors often use words like *said*, *exclaimed*, or *replied* to show who is talking.

- **Following the lines**—when speakers change, the words of the new speaker are indented and on the next line.

- **Matching words with a character**—some characters speak in distinctive ways, or say things that match their motivations.

Directions: Look at the conversation below. Use the pictures to point to who is saying what.

"This looks like a perfect place to build my web," said the spider.

"Oh, no! A spider is moving in!" wailed a passing butterfly.

"What was that? Who said that?"

"Oh—um, I want to welcome you to the neighborhood. Pleased to meet you."

"Pleased to meet you?" replied the spider. "I'll be even more pleased to eat you!"

FIGURE 5–2.

Moderate Level of Support. For students who needed a little less support, I gave them the character pictures but not the highlighted text. These students quickly showed that they had a stronger understanding of the flow of conversation.

"Where do we point when it's just the narrator speaking?" Samantha asked.

"Maybe we should just put our hand to the side," Anna responded.

"No, I'm going to write an *N* for narrator, and point to that," Samantha said. Other students in the group followed suit. I found this very interesting. In the last group, keeping a finger pointing to the previous character wasn't a problem. But this group of students didn't like pointing to a character who wasn't technically speaking, which revealed a different level of understanding.

As with the other group, I modeled by reading aloud and then set the students to read on their own. Because they did not have the additional support of the highlighted text, I knew that there might be some areas of trouble. "As you read on your own, I'll be listening in. I'd like you to do two things when you finish. First, summarize the conversation in a sentence or two. Also, find the part of the conversation that you think is trickiest to understand. We'll discuss these tricky parts later." Not only did I ask this group to make the macro-level connection, but I also challenged them to self-monitor their comprehension.

Low Level of Support. Sometimes, teachers decide that advanced students don't need the rich instruction, the guided lessons, or the scaffolding that less proficient readers need. After all, these students read well. They have pronounced reading tastes and can explain what they do and do not understand. But denying these students the opportunity to use physical props or rich activities is just asking for trouble. Because when Natalie came back to the guided reading table, her first question was, "Do we get mousey pictures too?"

I had considered dispensing with the pictures for this group. I was confident in their ability to follow the conversation and I was hoping to move them forward to the next level of inference. Luckily, I had chosen to make the pictures for this group after all. All students, regardless of their reading level, enjoy concrete activities and physical props. "Sure, you'll be getting pictures," I said.

"As we look at this conversation, what spots do you think will be tricky?" I asked the students, when we were ready to begin.

At my question, they started to page through the section. "I think the hardest part will be where the conversation just goes back and forth," Bria said, indicating a section of about ten lines in which there were no speaker tags.

"Yeah, that's confusing," Brendan agreed.

"How can we use the pictures to help us figure out who is talking?" I asked.

The group decided to read the lines with a partner and point to the different pictures as the conversation switched. Because this group was more aware of their comprehension and knew when they did or did not understand, they could take the lead in figuring out the tricky parts of the text and devising strategies for understanding. "After you and your partner read, I'd like you to try to summarize the entire conversation between Mr. Ages and Mrs. Frisby in just one or two sentences," I told them and then listened in on their reading.

Next Steps

Over the next few days, we continued working on making bridging inferences to figure out which character was speaking in dialogue. I knew that the strategies were taking hold when I noticed that Julie had written down the names of characters from her book in her reading journal.

"What's this for?" I asked, although I had a hunch.

"Oh," she said. "That's like what we did with the mice. I wrote down the names of the characters so that I can keep track of who is talking when they have a conversation."

When students use strategies spontaneously, teachers know that instruction has worked. "I'd like you to share your strategy with the rest of the class," I told Julie, who grinned and agreed. We were on our way to making sense of conversations.

When an Inference Depends on a Single Detail: Inferring with a Critical Fact

Figuring out multiple referents and understanding dialogue are just two types of text-based bridging inferences. These inferences are needed to build cohesion of the text. However, other text-based inferences are necessary for students to understand what happened in a text—and what might happen next.

There is a saying for writers that goes like this: If you introduce a knife in Act 1, you'd better use that knife in Act 5. In other words, if a writer draws the reader's attention to a particular detail at the beginning of a story, then that detail should be important for the end of the story.

Literature is filled with examples of these "critical details" that the author plants at the outset of a novel. The story of Elya Yelnats' promise to Madame Zeroni in *Holes* (Sacher 2000), Voldemort's malfunctioning *Avada Kedavra* curse in *Harry Potter and the Goblet of Fire* (Rowling 2000), the vanished great-uncle in *The Spiderwick Chronicles: The Field Guide* (DiTerlizzi and Black 2003)—none of these wonderful clues make sense if they are forgotten by the reader. Even when they are remembered, there is an active process that readers need to animate in order to make the inference.

Teaching About Critical Details

Some groups of students need more instruction in working with critical facts. I wrote the passage "Buying Jewelry" (Figure 5–3) to be a brief introduction to this skill.

This lesson is modeled on a 1993 study by Philip Winne, Lorraine Graham, and Leone Prock. In this study, struggling readers worked one-on-one with an adult to read texts conducive to making inferences based on a critical fact. The student was asked to make an inference based on the story and received immediate explanatory feedback about whether this inference was or was not supported by the story. According to the study, students who received explicit feedback improved at answering inference questions (Winne, Graham, and Prock 1993).

Here's how I adapted the study for classroom use. I gave copies of the story and the questions to the students. I read the story aloud to them and then asked them to complete the questions independently. The first question is the inference question, requiring the student to put the rule and the critical fact together to make an inference. The next three questions elicit the problem statement, rule, and critical fact from students. This ensures that students actually remember these details. The last question probes for distracting information given in the text.

After students had a chance to think about their answers, I projected a transparency of the text. Then, I went through the questions and we discussed the answers—but not in the order that they are listed. First, we talked about questions 2–5. I used a highlighter to show students where the answers could be found in the text. Finally, we returned to the first question, and I showed students how we could use the details from the other questions to form the inference.

Helping students make inferences based on critical facts is one of the most effective interventions I've used with readers. As they tried to make a logical guess about a passage, underlined text clues that helped them to form the inference, and got immediate feedback about their thinking, they became actively engaged in the learning process.

Conclusion

Inferences can be confusing. A teacher can become lost in the jungle of all of the different kinds of inferences, each of which places a slightly different demand on the reader. However, all inferences share a common trait: they all depend on details in the text.

Text-based inferences, which include bridging inferences and critical fact inferences, are important for students to understand. But many students fail to notice the details they need to use to form these inferences. By helping students notice the details of multiple referents and dialogue, teachers can help them better understand what is going on in a text.

Buying Jewelry

Anne and Brent were shopping for a present for their mother's birthday. "Mom said that she likes silver jewelry best," Anne said. Anne loved jewelry and had at least thirty different pairs of earrings.

"That sounds good to me," said Brent. "Let's go to the jewelry counter."

The two children went to the jewelry counter. They had to walk through the clothing department, by the candy section, and by the shoe department. "I need a new pair of shoes," Brent said.

"Not right now," Anne laughed. "We have to get Mom's present first."

They arrived at the jewelry counter. There was a display of many different kinds of jewelry—earrings, necklaces, pins, and bracelets. But there were only three items that Anne and Brent could afford.

"Here's a gold pin," Anne said. "It has a flower on it. Mom likes flowers."

"And here's a silver bracelet with blue stones," Brent said.

"The last thing we can afford is this black bead necklace," Anne said.

The clerk walked over to them. "Can I help you?" she asked.

1. What piece of jewelry do you think Brent and Anne chose? Why?

2. What did Anne and Brent go to the store to buy?

3. What kind of jewelry did their mother like best?

4. What kind of jewelry could Brent and Anne choose from?

5. What did Brent want to buy as they walked to the jewelry department?

FIGURE 5–3.

What about the inferences that depend more on a reader's prior knowledge? What about the rich, sensory inferences of visualization? These are the kinds of inferences that will be discussed in the next chapters.

Teaching About Details with Text-Based Inferences

- There are many different kinds of inferences.

- Text-based inferences are based on information in the text.

- Less skilled readers have problems with anaphoric relationships or dealing with multiple referents in a text.

- Many young readers have trouble using text clues to figure out who is speaking in dialogue.

- Teaching multiple groups with the same grade-level text can be effective, as long as the instruction is tailored to meet the students' needs.

- A specific kind of text-based inference is based on a "rule" given in a passage and a "critical fact" that relates to the rule.

- With specific feedback, students can become more proficient with text-based inferences.

6 READER-BASED INFERENCES

I'll never forget the experience of sharing Chris Van Allsburg's book *The Stranger* with third graders during my student teaching experience (Van Allsburg 1986). In the story, a stranger is accidentally hit by a farm truck and loses his memory. The family takes him in. As the weeks progress, it becomes clear that something is amiss: the leaves stay green and the temperatures stay warm, even though the season should be changing. Who is the mysterious stranger? How is he affecting the weather?

At the end of the story, the stranger leaves, and the next day the farm experiences its first frost. As I finished the story, I looked expectantly at the students. "Who was the stranger?" I asked.

They just stared at me.

I tried again. "Why do you think the frost only came after the stranger left? Who was he?"

And once again, they just stared at me.

Like most of Chris Van Allsburg's books, the secret of *The Stranger* can be unlocked with an inference. By combining the text clues with prior knowledge, a reader can figure out that the mysterious stranger must be Jack Frost. But the students I was reading to had never heard of Jack Frost. Without knowledge of this particular detail, they could not make the inference, and the story really didn't make much sense. These students could not make the reader-based inference necessary for understanding the story. As you'll see, reader-based inferences are vital for reading and enjoying text. It's no wonder that a study found strong correlations between inferring skill and overall reading comprehension (Cain, Oakhill, and Bryant 2004).

The Details of Rreader-Based Inferences

A reader-based inference depends on both the reader's prior knowledge and text clues. Let's put this together with the text-based inferences from the previous chapter. Text-based inferences depend largely on a reader's procedural knowledge of reading. Using clues from the text to match pronouns to antecedents requires a reader to use knowledge about the reading task but does not require a reader to activate a schema or pull from prior knowledge. These inferences are made at a fairly shallow level of processing, usually at the textbase. The reader-based inferences of this chapter, however, require richer, deeper connections. The inferences will vary based on what experiences and knowledge a reader brings to the text. These inferences do not only rely on simple procedural knowledge but also pull from a reader's declarative knowledge and are made at the level of the situation model (Winne, Graham, and Prock 1993).

Understanding how this prior knowledge is stored in the brain can help us consider the process of making reader-based inferences. The term *schema* is often used to describe how knowledge is structured in the mind. With my students, I like to compare schemas to file folders. Just like a file folder, a schema is a collection of all a reader's general experiences and knowledge about a concept or topic. Information can be added to a schema, just like new papers can be put in a folder. And the schema can be modified, like rearranging the papers in the folder.

When I first read *The Stranger*, for example, I pulled on my schema to infer that the stranger is Jack Frost. I can imagine my *Jack Frost* schema as built upon the silly rhymes and stories of childhood, a song that we learned for chorus, and images of the lacy frost designs on a windowsill. The file folder metaphor is not completely accurate in describing the dynamic nature of schemas. My *Jack Frost* schema fits entirely inside the *mythical creatures* schema and overlaps with my schema for *autumn*. Closely related schemas can overlap, whole schemas can fit inside of other schemas, and a concept can be represented in multiple ways in multiple schemas (Nuthall 1999b).

How do we use the information from our schemas to form inferences? In simple terms, something in the text activates background knowledge stored in long-term memory. That background knowledge, combined with information from the text, is encoded in memory. That is, a reader-based inference synthesizes information from prior knowledge and details from the text. The inference is usually remembered just as well as what was literally in the text.

The information in schemas is usually rich and vivid. Most of our knowledge, after all, comes from our real-life experiences, so memories of these experiences are represented in relevant schemas (Graesser, Singer, and Trabasso 1994). Consider *eating at the school cafeteria*. Most teachers have a wealth of background knowledge on the subject, from personal experience as a student and a teacher to more generic knowledge about how the cafeteria operates, cost considerations, and the importance of school nutrition programs. When you read about a story taking place in a school cafeteria, you can bring all the details and experiences you have accrued from your long-term memory to your working memory. This information is available on the spot for you to make inferences as they are necessary.

When the background information is not rich and vivid, inferring can be more difficult. Perhaps this explains why historical fiction has been such a tough sell in my classroom lately. The students do not have well-developed knowledge of historical events. Even though they may encounter words and phrases that should activate long-term memories, they cannot retrieve rich background knowledge, which means that they fail to make key inferences.

To make the huge topic of reader-based inferences more manageable, I deal with them in several different chapters. In the remainder of this chapter, we'll look at reader-based inferences as they relate to analyzing and understanding characters. In Chapter 7, we'll consider visualizing as an extended reader-based inference. And the inferences that are necessary for comprehending expository text will be discussed in Chapter 9.

A Pathway to Inferences: Learning About a Character

One of my favorite parts of reading stories is learning about a character. If students learn to connect with a character, they can be pulled into books as they experience a character's struggles, triumphs, and setbacks. But many students fail to make a meaningful connection with the characters in the books they read. I think this is partly due to an inability to keep up with the inferring demands of more challenging books.

Reader-based inferences are necessary for readers to make predictions about what characters will do, learn about what characters are like, or resolve inconsistencies between what a character does and what that same character might say. But these inferences require the reader to draw on a strong supply of background knowledge including experiences with people, knowledge about different traits and emotions, and knowledge of how stories work. Many intermediate students simply don't have this background.

As you have probably noticed throughout this book, one of the main concerns of teaching reading in the intermediate grades is helping students deal with the new demands of increasingly difficult text. Students are going from text that is considerate and explicit to text that requires more from the reader. If students don't have help in learning to cope with this kind of text, they will become disenchanted with reading and miss out on a world of literature. They will also miss out on the joys of reading subtle stories that gradually reveal their secrets.

Many teachers notice that students are drawn to series. Every few years, another popular series hits the shelves, and students read book after book that features the same characters and the same kinds of conflicts. These books are predictable in that they often begin with a chapter that introduces the characters. Right now, my fourth graders devour books from the Judy Moody series during independent reading (McDonald 2000). This series even includes a page that shows pictures of all of the characters and how they relate to one another. When students open up a Judy Moody book, or a book about her younger brother Stink, they are cocooned in a safe little reading world of familiar characters.

As students move from supportive early chapter books to more demanding text, however, they must emerge from this safe cocoon. In order for a reader to build a relationship with a character, a series of inferences must be made. The reader must pick up on scores of little details that slowly unlock the secrets of what the character is like. Instead of having an instant friend, a relationship must be built, piece by piece. Students who are part of a reading community, and can talk about their books with other children and adults, learn to make this transition and love books that yield their secrets slowly.

Without support to help them learn to make inferences with more challenging text, some students decide that books are no fun. Over the course of several years, I developed ways to help these students use the details of what they read to make important inferences about characters. In the next section, we'll examine what some of these key inferences entail; then we'll look at strategies and activities for the classroom.

Using Details to Make Inferences About Characters

> The teacher walked into the school cafeteria. It was the first day of school, and she had forgotten to pack a lunch.

Readers need to learn about a character's goals to understand a story. In the excerpt above, most readers will pull on their schema for *lunch* and *school cafeteria* to make an inference about why the teacher went into the cafeteria. It seems so obvious—the teacher went into the cafeteria to buy a lunch, since she had forgotten hers at home. In novels, concepts about character's goals often become much more complex, as the different goals of different characters become layered throughout the plot.

> "What will you have?" asked the cafeteria worker.
> "I think I'll try the snack wrap, plus some chips and some fruit," Ms. Trasser said. "Oh, and I'm so sorry that I forgot to send down a lunch count this morning. I promise to remember tomorrow. I send it down before the announcements, right?"
> "That's right," smiled the cafeteria worker, handing the tray to the teacher. "Don't worry about it. Dessert?"
> "Oh—not today, thank you," Ms. Trasser replied. Her long red fingernails contrasted sharply with the bland beige of the tray.

Readers don't make inferences based on every possible piece of information. For example, why did the cafeteria worker ask Ms. Trasser what she would have? Well, since she worked in the cafeteria, she probably wanted to do her job, and she wanted to do her job to get money. But this inference isn't necessary for understanding the story line as it is written, and so most readers will not spend time considering it.

There is also the question of why Ms. Trasser chose to skip dessert. From the given information, an adult reader might infer that Ms. Trasser is on a diet, or avoiding sweets. Suppose another sentence had been added before the teacher's refusal: "She eyed the congealed brown glop suspiciously." Drawing on your prior knowledge of cafeterias and pudding, you might infer that Ms. Trasser didn't think the dessert looked very appetizing.

It's easy for an adult reader to keep track of a character's goals and intentions throughout a simple story like this. However, students often have difficulty with this. When a character's goals are not explicitly stated, students often have trouble figuring out explanations for why a character might engage in an action (Sundbye 1987). This can interfere with their understanding of the whole story. If a reader does not understand why a character made a particular choice or engaged in a particular course of action, then that reader might not understand subsequent events or learn new information about what a character is like.

> After Ms. Trasser paid, she turned to leave the cafeteria. An especially fast first grader ran in front of her right at that moment. Ms. Trasser's tray flipped in the air and made a loud "bang" against the hard linoleum floor.
>
> "Oh, no," Ms. Trasser moaned. She started to exhale, but caught herself sharply and looked around the crowded room. She had no idea where the mops were kept. Instead, she knelt down and tried to clean up as best she could with her flimsy napkin.

Here, another reader-based inference must be made. How does Ms. Trasser feel at this moment? Inferring a character's emotional state at different points in the story is very important for comprehension, especially because a character's emotions might lead to future actions. In this example, the reader might infer that Ms. Trasser feels upset and embarrassed at dropping her tray. Because she feels this way, and because she does not know where the mops are, she kneels down and tries to clean up the mess herself. This is what I like to call a *layered inference*, one inference that depends upon another. A reader who misses the first inference will also miss the second.

Does it seem strange to you that Ms. Trasser, a teacher, would have no idea where the mops are kept in the cafeteria? And why is she so upset at spilling a little food? These details might be activating a *first-year teacher* schema in your mind. If this is Ms. Trasser's first day of her first year, it is perfectly logical for her to respond to this minor problem with such embarrassment. Most of us in the classroom have an especially well-developed knowledge structure for *first-year teacher* that can allow us to make many inferences.

But suppose that, in the next sentence, it were to be revealed that this is Ms. Trasser's seventh year of teaching in the building. Would this information seem odd to you? Would it cast Ms. Trasser's problems with the mop and the lunch count in a different light? This information about characters is being processed at the level of the situation model. As new information about characters is revealed, readers make updates to their situation model, spending more time reading sentences that are inconsistent with previous information than reading sentences that fit with what they have already learned (Albrecht and O'Brien 1993). This makes sense, especially when I consider my own reading habits. Like Harry Potter, I was shocked when I learned, in *Order of the Phoenix*, that his father, James, had been a bit of an arrogant bully (Rowling 2003). This information didn't fit in with what I thought I knew, and I had to do some mental updating to make sense of it.

Let's return to the scenario that has Ms. Trasser cast as a first-year teacher.

> The principal appeared at her side. "Don't worry about it," she said. "I'll ask the custodian to clean it up."
>
> "Oh," said Ms. Trasser, flustered. She stood up and pushed her flaming red hair out of her eyes."I'm so sorry. It's so embarrassing."
>
> "Look, they've already made you another tray," the principal said, pointing to the cafeteria line. "Go and enjoy your lunch. Heaven knows you don't have much time."
>
> "I'll show you the way to the faculty room," said Mrs. Leon, who was also coming through the line. "There's fresh peach pie there today. Just the pickup you need to get through the afternoon."
>
> "Go ahead," smiled the principal encouragingly, and Ms. Trasser went and picked up the tray.

Besides inferring characters' goals and emotions, it is also important to make some judgments about their character traits. Character traits serve as good predictors for how characters will eventually act. But few authors state traits directly. Instead, we need to rely on what the authors "show" us of their characters—how the characters act, what they say, what they think, and what others say about them.

What inference could you make about the principal? Well, she seems quite kind and caring, because she told Ms. Trasser not to worry about cleaning up, and to go ahead and enjoy her lunch. You probably have a schema for *principal* or *administrator* that you can use as a basis of comparison for the principal in this story. You also have to pull from a schema that defines what each of these traits means. For instance, the schema for *kind* probably includes ideas like caring for others, helping people, saying nice words, and so forth.

For all that it had characters with goals, traits, and emotions, the preceding example probably left you feeling a little unsatisfied. The main character didn't experience a struggle; there was no conflict; there was no story. As in the previous chapter, when I urged you to take micro-level interventions back to a macro-level understanding of the story, now I urge you to take inferences about a character back to a story. It's fun to have students work with little pieces of text to make inferences about a character's goals, emotions, and traits. Wherever you can, be sure that these inferences add up to something bigger.

> She struggled with her emotions. Yes, she wanted to eat in the faculty room with the other teachers. But she had also been hoping for some quiet time alone at lunch. And the thought of peach pie made her cringe.
>
> "I'll be right back," Ms. Trasser promised the other teachers, once she had arrived in the faculty room. She rushed outside to a quiet, unseen alcove between the building and the parking lot. Concentrating very hard, she focused on one tiny patch of grass, exhaled once, and breathed a perfect line of fire into the air. The patch of grass was completely incinerated.
>
> "Now I'll be able to get through the afternoon," she whispered to herself, "as long as I don't eat anything sweet." She had known that it would be hard to keep her secret, once she started teaching. But no one, no one could know her true identity. No one could know that she was really a dragon. Fighting the urge to let loose her wings and fly away, Ms. Trasser turned and went to go back into the building.
>
> Across the playground, a little girl stared. "Mikey," she breathed, "I think we need to be extra-special good this afternoon."

With the addition of this new information, some of the details from the previous portions have new meaning. Inferences need to be updated and new inferences made. Keeping track of a character's goals, emotions, and traits is vital for understanding text. What were once disconnected goals, emotions, and traits now make a little more sense.

Teaching Reader-Based Inferences to Help Students Understand Character

Teaching students to make inferences about characters helps them gain a deeper understanding of stories. One of the first steps is to bring them in on the inferring process. If students understand how they use their prior knowledge to make inferences, then they can take control of the process. To start instruction, then, I guide students toward tracing the origins of their inferences.

There is a strong similarity between reader-based inferences and text-based inferences. In text-based inferences, the reader combines a rule from the text with a critical fact that is also given in the text to generate an inference. In reader-based inferences, the process is quite similar. However, instead of coming from the text, the rule that governs the inference comes from the reader's prior knowledge.

Many students draw on their prior knowledge but are not aware of it. The link between their long-term memory and their working memory seems to operate at a superstealth mode, leaving these students with the ability to make inferences but incapable of explaining them. To help students become aware of their inferring, I like to start with very simple, very concrete "snippets," little pieces of text that invoke an inference. I know that students have an easier time generating background knowledge related to familiar experiences. Therefore, the ideas in these snippets are quite familiar.

I compiled some of my favorite snippets on the Making Inferences page (Figure 6–1). When I introduced the idea, students were confident at first.

"As a reader, it's important to make inferences based on your own background knowledge and clues from the text. Let's take a look at the first sentence. "Luke dove for the sundae, but it was too late." Based on this sentence, what do you think happened to the sundae?"

Mark offered to act the sentence out. He jumped for an imaginary sundae, even yelling a slow motion "Nooo!" as it supposedly slipped from his grasp. "Well, I dive for the sundae, but I'm too late. So the sundae must have fallen down."

"How do you know that?" I asked.

"If he was diving for it, I guess it would have been falling," Tasha said. "You wouldn't dive for a sundae unless it was going to fall."

"Or a seagull was about to get it," Matt interjected.

A seagull? Where did this come from? As you might know, this is a common problem. Sometimes less skilled readers will pull on any background knowledge to form an inference—even if the background knowledge does not fit with the text. A comment about a thieving seagull is good for a quick laugh during reading group. But I can't allow this line of reasoning to persist.

"I think Tasha is on the right track," I put in.

"So I see the sundae smashed on the floor," Mark said. "I've spilled ice cream before, and it makes a big mess."

The first inference went well, as did the second. At the third sentence, the students started to show some problems. "Bernice and Kirsten looked at the kitchen in dismay. Flour and eggs were dumped on the floor. Pots and pans were all about. 'This will take forever,' moaned Bernice."

Making Inferences

An *inference* is a logical guess that you make based on your own background knowledge and clues from the text.

Directions: Readers make inferences all the time. Read the example and answer the questions.

Luke dove for the sundae, but he was too late.

What was Luke trying to do? _____

What happened to the sundae? _____

How do you know? _____

Jackie shivered on the playground, wishing that she had brought a coat.

What is the weather like? _____

How do you know? _____

Bernice and Kirsten looked at the kitchen in dismay. Flour and eggs were dumped on the floor. Pots and pans were all about. "This will take forever," moaned Bernice.

What are Bernice and Kirsten trying to do? _____

How do they feel about it? _____

Andrew and Cody were excited to go snowboarding. "I hope I don't fall," Andrew said nervously. "This hill is huge."
   Cody said, "There's the instructor. He'll show us what to do."

Have Andrew and Cody been snowboarding before? _____

How do you know? _____

FIGURE 6–1.

"What do you think Bernice and Kirsten are doing?" I asked.

Their understanding was, at first, hampered by the word *dismay*. "What does *dismay* mean?" Tasha asked.

I explained briefly, noting that I needed to revisit this word in upcoming days.

"Well," said Mark, "if they were in the kitchen, and there were pots and pans, it sounds like the kitchen was a mess."

Matt nodded. "And they were in dismay because they probably had to, like, clean it."

"I bet they're really upset," Tasha said. "I know that I hate to clean the kitchen."

Alejandra spoke up for the first time. "I wonder if they have a little sister who made the mess," she said shyly. "My sister always messes up things."

Step by step, snippet by snippet, the students were starting to be able to trace the origins of their inferences. Notice how important details are for tracing an inference. Students need to be able to access the details from their schemas that led them to form the inference.

Using Details to Infer Emotions

How do characters feel at different parts of the story? In order to infer a character's emotions, students need to draw on the "rule" of their experiences with different feelings and match these with the critical facts of what is happening in the story. These inferences are important, because a character's emotions at a certain time are often the motivations for their actions later.

But students showed two main problems with inferring a character's emotions. For one, they avoided using specific emotion words, clinging instead to generic words like *mad* and *sad*. For another, they sometimes failed to distinguish between traits and emotions. I knew that we would need to work on these problem areas.

Whole-Group Lesson

A conversation about inferring emotions actually begins with morning meeting. "I'd like everyone to tell us how they're feeling today, in the form of a weather report," I told the students. "For example, if you're feeling happy today, say that you are sunny." Kids smiled and laughed, and we went around the circle, with weather forecasts ranging from "partly cloudy" to "chance of a tornado later." Uh-oh!

Later, during the whole-group reading lesson, this gave us a context for reference. "Everyone has feelings," I told the class. "Our feelings change over time. For example, Brad told us in morning meeting that he was feeling stormy. Brad, do you still feel that way?"

Brad looked up in surprise. "Actually, no," he said. "I got to go to tutoring in kindergarten, which made me feel pretty happy."

I couldn't have asked for a better lead-in to the lesson. "Usually, our feelings will change in reaction to things that happen to us. Today we're going to talk about how we can infer a character's emotions based on what happens in the text. Remember, when we infer, we think about what we already know, and then we think about what happens in the text. When we combine those, we get an inference."

I wrote the words *angry, happy,* and *sad* on the board. These are the words my students use most frequently. I decided to start with these and then expand to more specific words. Then, I gave each small group of students a different Inferring a Character's Emotions card (Figure 6–2) to read, with the directions that they were to match the scenario on the card with an emotion, saying, "I want you to make sure you are thinking about what these feelings actually mean. What does it mean to be angry? How would the event that your group has cause a character to be angry?"

As I walked around to listen to the conversations, I was pleased to hear the level of rich detail. Clearly, students were drawing on their background knowledge. "I saw someone that had had a tornado go through their home," Andrea said. "It looked horrible. I think I would be sad."

"We thought there would be a tornado at our house," Carly said. "That was scary enough."

These scenarios and emotions were not meant to be challenging. Instead, I wanted to choose familiar topics to ensure that they would draw on rich stores of background knowledge. After a few moments of small-group discussion, the students shared their answers with the large group.

"Now, let's talk about these events," I said. "I think there's something wrong here. You say that the character who loses an ice cream cone is sad, and the character who loses a house to a tornado is sad too. Which character would be sadder?"

Obviously, students responded that the character who lost the house would be sadder. "We need a better word than *sad*," Bria said.

"Absolutely!" I agreed. "If you can think of some more specific words for *sad*, write those down. I'll also be sending Bria around with a paper that lists some different words." I designed the Emotion Words paper (Figure 6–3) as a tool for the students who don't have a large store of words at their command. Forming an inference is taxing enough—forming an inference and coming up with specific words can be overwhelming!

"I think that Marya would be heavyhearted," Ian called out, after looking at the list. "I like that word. Heavyhearted."

"And if I were Eli, I would be furious," Shannon said.

When students are led to see that a strategy is ineffective, they are far more willing to take an alternate course. This class saw that using the same words to describe a character's emotions in response to vastly different events wasn't working. They attacked the Emotion Words paper eagerly, looking through the list for words that conveyed their ideas more clearly.

Inferring a Character's Emotions: Situations

Directions: Cut out cards. Give a situation card to each group or individual.

You get a three-scoop chocolate dream ice cream cone with extra sprinkles, only to have it topple over and fall as soon as you leave the ice cream store.	You find out that you have won a writing contest and will be getting $100 as a prize.
Your little brother has completely demolished your room, tearing down every poster and taking apart your three thousand–piece Lego models.	Marya's home was destroyed by a tornado, leaving her family with nothing.
Eli was fired from his job as a cashier because the boss' daughter was stealing money from the cash register.	On Eric's trip to the beach, he found out that there was a kid staying next door who was his own age and interested in the same things.
Breanna stayed up late to work on an exciting science project and made a new discovery.	Sandy's next-door neighbor threw Sandy's backpack into a muddy puddle.

FIGURE 6–2.

Emotion Words

As you describe your character's emotions, try using these more specific words. Use a dictionary or thesaurus to help you understand them.

	Sad	Happy	Angry	Confused
Less intense	melancholy	content	flustered	puzzled
	blue	relieved	annoyed	intrigued
			aggrieved	
	depressed	joyful	indignant	curious
			exasperated	
	sorrowful	pleased	upset	perplexed
	tearful		inflamed	
		cheerful	mad	lost
	heavyhearted		furious	
	grief-stricken	ecstatic	livid	adrift
More intense	hopeless	jubilant	enraged	bewildered

FIGURE 6–3.

Later, in guided reading groups, we revisited the whole-group lesson. I asked students to bring their lists of emotion words with them to the meeting. "Let's talk about how we can infer a character's feelings from events that happened in the story we read yesterday," I said. Even though different groups were working on different stories at the time, we could look through each story and talk about a character's emotions. For my less skilled readers, I had made note cards listing different events so that they could match the event to a feeling. For other groups, I asked students to generate the events that we used. Throughout the lesson, I urged students to try to use different emotion words from the whole-group lesson. In order for these words to be available for future inferring, students needed repeated experience with them, enough experience that would enable them to generate a rule for that emotion.

I knew that this lesson had been successful when Mara came in from recess a few weeks later and declared, "Mrs. Kissner, I'm just bewildered!" She proceeded to tell a story of the incomprehensible actions of second graders. Mara clearly had a rule for the set of experiences that defines the word *bewildered*.

Using Details to Infer Character Traits

Just like a character's emotions, a character's traits can also be used to determine goals and future actions. Readers need to infer the traits of characters to understand what those characters are really like.

However, when I asked my students to find traits of characters in stories that we read, they often produced emotions instead. Although emotions change frequently in response to the events in a story, a trait usually stays the same.

Emotions Versus Traits

I help students differentiate between emotions and traits in several ways. One fun activity is to do a word sort with emotions versus traits. Give students a page with different emotions mixed in with different traits—ten of each works well. Then, have students cut out the words and sort them into two piles, one labeled "emotions" and one labeled "traits." There are some words that will fit in both categories. The word *angry* is usually considered an emotion word. However, a character who snaps at everyone might also be considered to have the trait *angry*.

Read-aloud time is another opportunity to show students the difference between emotions and traits. While I am reading, we often discuss how characters might feel given certain events in the book. Then, we look at how the character's emotions change but the traits tend to stay the same.

Enhancing Background Knowledge About Traits

Students have other problems with inferring traits. To generate an inference about a character's traits, something in the text needs to trigger the reader's background knowledge and experiences related to different traits. So there are two different ways for an inference to fail: either the information in the text will not trigger the appropriate memories, or the reader does not have the necessary background knowledge.

Let's deal with the background knowledge problem first. Readers need to have a store of different character traits, and be able to match different actions with those traits. In other words, they need to have a rule for different traits. Some of the necessary knowledge can come from reading other texts, of course. Hopefully, most students will not have firsthand experience with someone who is evil. But any student who has seen his share of Disney movies has encountered a wide variety of evil characters. Students who read a great deal, as well as dedicated movie fans, have an advantage here. They have more knowledge of different characters and more knowledge of how different traits lead to different actions.

Even when students have the necessary background knowledge, they may still fail to make the inference. Something in the text has to set the whole process in motion. Readers have to be sensitive to certain trigger words that cause them to generate an inference. Proficient readers do this unconsciously. How could I help students become more sensitive to these triggers?

I chose a story that I felt had many opportunities to infer character traits for the main character. When I started the group, I told students that we would be reading the story to learn as much as we could about the main character. "As we read today, we want to infer some character traits of Aster. We want to see what she is like. To get us ready, let's try to make a list of as many character traits as we can think of." I wrote down the students' suggestions as they called them out. I wanted them to bring information related to character traits from long-term memory into working memory, and making a list of traits was a good way to do this.

Next, we read the story together. I stopped frequently for discussion about how recent sentences helped us to learn about Aster's traits. "How do I know when to think about what Aster is like? Imagine the author shining a flashlight over certain details. These are the important details that the reader is supposed to notice. If the author spends some time on an idea or a detail, chances are it is something important," I told them.

Because we had brainstormed traits at the beginning of the lesson, students had the necessary background knowledge in working memory to make the inferences about the main character's traits. As we worked through the story, I helped students recognize which words and phrases should trigger the inference process. With this support, readers of all levels were able to be successful.

Inferring from Dialogue

So far, we have looked at how readers can infer a character's emotions and traits and use those inferences to make predictions and judgments about a character's actions. The next section will connect one of the bridging inferences from the previous chapter with the reader-based inferences in this chapter.

As you probably remember, students need to make bridging inferences to figure out who is speaking in dialogue. In turn, understanding who is speaking can help a reader to use the dialogue to learn more about a story. Dialogue accomplishes three main purposes: it reveals character, it gives information, and it moves the story forward (Bauer 1992). In fact, when I am trying to breeze through a story, I'll often skip the rest of the description and just read the dialogue.

To help my readers make inferences from dialogue, it's fun to do a little acting. I enlist willing students to play some parts, and then we infer information about the characters together. Here are some of the sentences that we act out.

> "I'm really tired, but I have to get this room cleaned up," Mandy sighed.

"What do these words tell us about Mandy?" I asked the class.
"Well, she's tired," Lydia said.
"What could we infer about her? What could we learn about her traits?" I probed.
Janelle said, "She's tired, but she wants to finish. I think that's responsible."
Thomas added, "Persistence, too. It shows that."
To help students grasp the process that they used to make this inference, I asked Thomas for more information. "Could you explain that some more? Why does this show that she's persistent?"
Thomas answered by saying what he knew *persistence* meant—in other words, his rule for persistence. "Being persistent, isn't it like not giving up? And she's tired, so she wants to give up, but she's not going to."
With the next example, I directed students to work with a partner to identify a trait based on the dialogue. Some of them went back to their notebooks to refer to the list of traits that we had previously generated in guided reading.
Once students were getting the idea, I showed them a sentence in which the speaker tag also carries information.

> "I'm not going to study tonight," Mark snarled, "and I'm not going to study tomorrow night, either!"

Notice how the word *snarled* in the speaker tag carries a great deal of information. From it, the reader can infer that Mark is angry. "Is he angry about studying, I wonder?" Janelle mused.

"It sounds like he's dumb," Shannon added. "He doesn't ever want to study."

"I don't think we can say he's dumb," Patrick told her. "We don't know enough yet."

"You're not invited to my party," Amy said, laughing. "I don't think I want to hang around with you anymore."

"Wow, it sounds like she's mean," Jenny said.

"Why would she laugh as she said that?" Mara wondered.

"If I were another character in this story, I'd just say fine to Amy, because she doesn't sound like a very good friend," Carly pronounced.

Once students are proficient at looking at what they can learn from dialogue in isolation, they can begin analyzing the dialogue in stories they read. Instead of skipping dialogue, students will find that it yields a wealth of useful information. The Analyzing Dialogue page (Figure 6–4) is a useful tool for helping students look carefully at dialogue. Because it is generic and not linked to a particular story, it is a good choice for a time when guided reading groups are reading a variety of stories.

Once again, you can see how one inference can lead to another. The text-based bridging inference of determining who is talking leads a reader to form a reader-based inference.

Using Details to Infer a Character's Goals

Why does a character choose to act in a certain way? What causes a character's actions? Understanding a character's traits and emotions helps a reader understand the choices that a character makes. In turn, understanding the causes of a character's actions helps a story make sense as a whole.

Young readers, though, are not very good at understanding a character's motives. This isn't surprising. In my classroom, kids can't figure out why *anyone* does *anything*.

"Mrs. Kissner! I can't believe this! Shannon moved my metal box that I was keeping things in for my courtroom!" Lindsay wailed to me after recess one day. "And she did it *on purpose* because she knew it would make me mad!"

"Are you sure?" I asked. "Let's ask her." I beckoned to Shannon, who came right over. "Shannon, why did you move Lindsay's box?"

Shannon looked confused. "That box is Lindsay's? I didn't know that. I just moved it so I could use the table. It's on the floor over there."

"It is mine and I wanted it on the table, not on the floor!" Lindsay insisted.

"But I needed to use the table!" Shannon snapped back. "Why do you always accuse people of things, Lindsay? You know, there are other people here!"

Analyzing Dialogue

Dialogue from the Text	Who Said It	Purpose of the Dialogue
		____ Gives information ____ Shows what a character is like ____ Pushes the story forward Why:
		____ Gives information ____ Shows what a character is like ____ Pushes the story forward Why:
		____ Gives information ____ Shows what a character is like ____ Pushes the story forward Why:
		____ Gives information ____ Shows what a character is like ____ Pushes the story forward Why:

FIGURE 6–4.

Uh-oh. I could tell that a major confrontation was brewing. This confrontation developed from the fact that neither Lindsay nor Shannon could accurately read the other's motivations. Both of these students made inferences about the situation without carefully noting the details.

How many problems in our classrooms stem from this inability to understand why people do the things they do? Each day, I deal with at least one conflict like this. I think students have so much trouble understanding someone else's motivation because it requires a pretty strong inference. Students need to draw on clues from the situation at hand and their background knowledge to infer a reason for someone's actions. If a student's background knowledge is flawed or lacking, then the student will make an inappropriate inference.

Students' background knowledge, as formed by their experiences, figures prominently in how they attribute actions to various motivations. When students live in households in which people frequently act for power or revenge, they instantly look to these causes to explain the behavior of others. Students who do not have much experience with altruism as a motivation will have trouble understanding the concept. Not only will this affect their interactions with other students, but it will also affect their reading, as they interpret stories quite differently according to their preconceived ideas of how the world works.

Helping Students Understand the Details of Their Own Behavior
How can we help students understand the motivations of characters? One important step is to help them recognize their own motivations. Kids sometimes do things for reasons that even they don't understand. If they can't figure out what led them to a certain action, they'll definitely have problems understanding what led a character to an action.

Talking to kids about their motivations can happen naturally at different points throughout the day. When you notice kids doing certain things, ask them about their reasons. "Faviola, I noticed that you were playing with the kindergarteners at recess. I'm interested in why you chose to do that," I said to Faviola one afternoon, and I learned that she really liked playing with the younger kids. "Patrick, why do you leave your things lying out all over the floor?" I asked one afternoon in exasperation. Together, we worked out that Patrick was worried about missing his bus and rushed through the afternoon cleanup. This strategy works well with misbehavior, too. "Melissa, I know that you and Jen had a disagreement yesterday. Can you tell me how this relates to the rumors you were spreading at lunch?"

Thinking about the motivations for our actions can be useful in whole-group situations as well. "For this afternoon's question, I'd like you to think about something you did today, and explain why you did it." Answers ranged from picking up trash in the cafeteria to avoid getting in trouble, to cleaning out a desk because it feels nice to have a clean workspace, to rearranging the supplies cabinet for easier access. These experiences help students understand themselves as well as understand more of the actions of their classmates. They were trying to reason through the details of their day.

"Mrs. Kissner, I think this is Lindsay's paper, and I don't want her to think that I moved it just to annoy her," Shannon told me, two days later. "She always leaves her stuff on the table, though."

"What do you think would be the best thing to do?" I asked Shannon.

Shannon sighed. "Well, I guess I'll take it and put it neatly on her desk, and then I'll try to tell her as soon as I can. But I'm really not trying to mess with her."

"I think she'll understand," I assured Shannon. Not only had Shannon paused to consider the reasons for her own actions, but she was trying to forecast what Lindsay would think. Maybe harmony could reign, after all.

Layering Inference upon Inference with Character Goals

In previous sections, I mentioned how understanding a character's emotions and traits is important for making inferences about a character's goals. Characters act according to their goals, but also according to their traits and their emotional state. Someone who is angry might be expected to make very different decisions than someone who is calm, even if they are both operating with the same goals. Also, someone who is a cheerful, positive person will make different choices than someone who is negative. Consider this sentence.

> Ethan reached across the table and knocked over his sister's juice.

This poses a puzzle for the reader. Why did Ethan knock over the juice? What if the preceding sentence read like this?

> "That was a mean thing to say!" Ethan exclaimed.

In this case, the skilled reader automatically makes two inferences: that Ethan is angry at his sister and that this anger leads him to knock over the juice.

However, suppose the previous sentence had read like this instead.

> "It's fun to have a picnic in the park," Ethan said.

This sentence doesn't lead us to the inference that Ethan is angry, and so we are left with more of a question about Ethan's actions. A reader might even conclude that there is something else happening here that has not yet been revealed by the author. Perhaps there is a reason for Ethan's action. A preceding sentence like the next one would bring about that inference even more strongly.

"I hate it when yellow jackets attack us!" Ethan muttered.

In this case, the reader can infer that Ethan knocked over the juice because it had a yellow jacket in it. Clearly, the reason for Ethan's action changes depending on previous inferences. Each individual detail leads to an inference that is used to generate further inferences. A student who skips over details or does not activate prior knowledge can miss out on a great deal.

In my classroom, I've found that the best way to teach these layered inferences is through repeated exposure to text. The more stories that students encounter, the more background knowledge they will have available to use for future inferences. Through read-aloud, reading groups, and independent reading, students need to read stories in which characters have different motivations for their actions.

Understanding why characters act the way they do is not something that can be taught quickly and easily. However, understanding character motivation is an important kind of reader-based inference.

Conclusion

Reader-based inferences are a fascinating little corner of the reading world. A reader-based inference depends on what the reader already knows. When teaching reader-based inferences, it's important to consider the background knowledge that readers bring to the text. Readers often fail to generate inferences when they lack the necessary vocabulary or knowledge that matches a set of experiences. Students also fail to act on details in the text, missing important ideas that could guide their inferences. Instruction needs to build students' background knowledge and help them see when they should generate inferences.

Students can learn even more about making inferences by taking over the task of writing. In the next chapter, we'll look at how writing lessons about details can build students' inferring skills.

Teaching About Details with Reader-Based Inferences

- Reader-based inferences require a reader to draw on existing schemas.

- When students do not have the necessary background information about a topic in their schema, they may fail to make key inferences.

- Helping students to trace their inferences, or think about the details in their prior knowledge that helped them to make the inference, will help students become more aware of their own thinking process.

- Inferring the emotions of a character helps a reader understand the character's goals and motivations.

- Many students do not have a well-developed schema for complex emotions.

- Students also lack background knowledge related to character traits and how those traits are likely to influence further actions.

- Instead of skipping dialogue, readers should look at how dialogue can reveal character, give information, or move the story forward.

- Many inferences in a text are layered—that is, a reader needs to use information generated from one inference to make another inference.

7

THE IMPORTANCE OF
DETAILS IN VISUALIZING

One morning, as I was teaching about visualizing, Brendan interrupted me with a perceptive comment. "How can our brains do that?" he asked. "I mean, when I read, I'm thinking of a picture in my head, but I'm still reading. It's like I'm doing two things at once."

Visualizing is pretty amazing. We are incredibly lucky to be able to create these pictures in our minds. How can our brains do that? And how is visualizing important for reading?

Thinking about how visualizing works leads back to the three levels of text. Visualizations seem to happen at the deepest level of text, the situation model. Remember, this is the level in which ideas from the text interact with the reader's prior knowledge. The situation model is thought to have some perceptual qualities—that is, our feeling that we "see" the action in a well-written novel might actually be close to the truth (Fincher-Kiefer and D'Agostino 2004). When we're reading way down deep in a book, it's almost as if we've been transported to another place and time, where we can track a main character through time and space and note important objects and events, and where events are linked through causality.

Details are immensely important to visualizing. The author's details are the basis of our visualizations. By drawing our eyes to certain details, the author shows us what is important in the imagined world of the book. But the author's details are not all that is needed to build a visual image. At its core, visualizing is really a form of extended inference.

Think about it this way: an author never reveals every detail of a place in a description. This would make for some very dull reading. Instead, the author assumes that the reader will pull on appropriate background knowledge to build the image. An author might write, "A red barn towered over the fields and orchards." The author would not specify that the orchards are made up of trees or that the barn is made of wood; these details seem obvious.

Although the term *visualizing* is most often used to describe this process, it does not perfectly describe what happens at the situation level. Readers do not just "see" a picture in their minds. Authors can evoke feelings from all of the senses. With the sentence "The acrid scent of burning leaves drifted from the pasture," the reader can imagine not just the visual images of the barn, fields, and orchard, but also the smell of the burning leaves. With my students, I like to use the term *sensory images* as well as *visualizing*, so that they understand that they can understand that this is a process that involves all of the senses.

What is the purpose of visualizing in reading? Is it possible to be a competent reader and never form these kinds of visual images? Well, one can gain a literal understanding of the text, an understanding at the level of the textbase, without necessarily creating sensory images. But this would be a shallow, dull form of reading. I like to think that visualizing is an effective way to help readers attain the situation model. By forming these sensory images, students can experience what it is like to integrate their prior knowledge and new information from the text. Students can't understand the direction, "As you read, try to go deeper than just the words—integrate the words on the page with what you already know." I can only imagine how such a directive would go over in my classroom. But students can understand, "As you read, try to imagine yourself in the world that the author describes. Try to see the sights and hear the sounds."

Because it leads to such a deep level of processing, visualizing has been used in many interventions to improve reading comprehension. A 1986 study showed that helping students use mental imagery enhanced their self-monitoring and reading comprehension (Gambrell and Bales 1986). In addition, creating mental images also helps readers remember important details about new topics (Willoughby et al. 1997). Visualizing enables kids to become engaged with a text, leading to better comprehension and more active processing.

In this chapter, we examine how to help students draw on prior knowledge to visualize. Then we look at how to help students pay close attention to text details as they visualize and change their visual images as information changes.

Drawing on Schema

In order to visualize a scene, a reader needs to pull on existing schemas. We can think about our schemas as existing in a hierarchy, with more specific schemas at the bottom and more generalized schemas at the top. Schemas can also overlap, with different concepts being represented in multiple ways. For example, think about a *petting zoo*. Images and experiences related to a petting zoo might be associated with a more general *zoo* schema. But because the animals at a petting zoo are often farm animals, the petting zoo might also be represented with the general *farm* schema. These dynamic connections allow readers to think flexibly about related topics (Nuthall 1999a).

The process of visualizing requires readers to activate and pull from their existing schemas. Remember the file folder metaphor? Telling students to "open your file folders" is a concrete way to help them activate their schemas. Before reading a story that took place in China, for instance, I told students to open up their file folders of information about life in China. What's neat about schemas is that the process works both ways. Not only do readers draw from their existing schemas as they read, but they also add to their schemas. I loved the Little House on the Prairie books as a child (Wilder 1935). I'd never visited the prairie, but the details in the book made the vast expanses of grass seem real. I built a schema for the prairie.

A Lesson in Schema

To understand the classroom story that follows, take a brief moment to revisit your schema for the *Great Depression*. You might bring to mind images of the Dust Bowl, of people looking for work, of hobos and bread lines. I remember the books that I have read about that time, especially *No Promises in the Wind*, the story of two brothers' search for jobs and homes in the Midwest (Hunt 1970). I think of parks that were built by the Civilian Conservation Corps, Eleanor Roosevelt, and the New Deal. Like me, you probably have a fairly well-developed schema for the era.

When I started reading aloud Richard Peck's *A Long Way from Chicago*, I wanted students to notice how important details from a text could activate their prior knowledge (Peck 1998). In the first chapter of the book, Peck mentions the Great Depression. I knew that students had read some nonfiction about the Great Depression in the previous year. I paused in the story and posed a question. "Now, as readers, this should ring some bells in your heads. When you hear the words *Great Depression*, what do you think of?"

There was a moment of silence in the classroom. Jessica tentatively raised a hand. "I think it's kind of like someone who feels really bad, who is feeling depressed."

Several other students nodded. Hm, I thought. "Does anyone have any other connections? Maybe something about a time in history?"

"Ooh, ooh!" called out Thomas, urgently raising his hand. "Maybe something really bad happened, like a natural disaster, and everyone was depressed about it. So it was a great depression."

I knew that students had read about the Great Depression. Somehow, though, this information had escaped from their brains. They were not able to activate their schemas, and so they would not be able to make mental images or key inferences.

To help students understand how they can generate mental images—and invoke schemas—with just a few words from text, I developed the Setting Schema page (Figure 7–1). The purpose is to help students understand how they use their schemas to create mental images.

The activity is quite simple. First I distributed the papers to the students, and then I showed them a series of words on the overhead projector. For the first scenario, I started out with *barn*. Then, I added the words

Setting Schema

As you read, you need to be ready to activate your schema for various ideas and concepts that appear in the text. Starting a new story is like landing on an alien planet. You need to work quickly to figure out where you are, what's happening, and who is important.

Directions: Watch as different words are displayed. What pictures do you see in your mind? For each scenario, write a prediction of what you might encounter in the text.

Scenario #1

What I picture in my mind: _____

_____

Scenario #2

What I picture in my mind: _____

_____

What this story might be about: _____

_____

Scenario #3

What I picture in my mind: _____

_____

What this story might be about: _____

_____

Words or events you might expect: _____

_____

Scenario #4

What I picture in my mind at first: _____

_____

How this picture changes: _____

_____

FIGURE 7–1.

father and son and *planting season*. Finally, I added what I thought would be quite a loaded word: *redcoats*.

"Wow," Thomas said. "Even with just a few words, I can make a picture in my mind." This is just what I had hoped for. Later, we would work on refining mental images and keeping them congruent with the text. For now, I was happy that they were creating any images at all.

After I displayed the words, I gave students some time to consider their mental images, and then I allowed them to share their ideas in groups. The students were eager to talk about their mental images. "I see a dad and his kid, and they're by the barn, and it's springtime," Andrea said.

"Yeah," added Samantha. "And they're both wearing jackets, because it's still chilly. Red jackets."

Interesting, I thought. As I circulated around the classroom, I discovered that only one group of students had attached any significance to the word *redcoats*. The other groups passed over this clue. They did not set their visualizations in the past, but took that detail and pushed it forward into the present. Just like the Great Depression detail, they skipped it entirely. Think of how this would affect their visualizing. These students would miss further details because they were not operating out of their *Revolutionary War* schema. If new information were presented in the text, these readers would not add it to their schema.

Caleb, Thomas, and Scott, who were all Boy Scouts, had visited Revolutionary War sites. Not only did they see the importance of the redcoats, but they were also able to explain it to their group. "Well, I see a 1700s barn housing redcoats in Massachusetts and the father and son are running away into danger," Caleb explained. Once the others boys had heard the explanation, they readily absorbed the idea into their own images. This is an example of how social interactions can change and reshape schemas (McVee, Dunmore, and Gavelek 2005). By talking about their mental images, these boys had altered their knowledge structure and were able to draw on new recollections and experiences to form a mental image. Thomas called me over. "Mrs. Kissner! I thought that it was just saying that their coats were red, but it was really like the Revolutionary War that we learned about last year. Isn't that cool?"

Because my lesson was mainly concerned with schemas and visualizing, I did not take the time to discuss how the word *redcoats* relates to the Revolutionary War. Instead, I called on different groups to share the sensory images they had created. I emphasized how I had heard different students talking about how their prior knowledge helped them to create pictures in their minds.

For the second scenario, I showed a completely different set of words. I began by revealing *saltwater* and *wooden ship*. This brought some sighs of recollection from the students. "Ah, saltwater! That makes me think of the beach," said Danielle, inhaling an imaginary sea breeze.

What I did next created an unusual result. Instead of reading aloud the next two words, *cannon* and *sails*, I simply displayed the words on the overhead projector. "I'd like you to think silently for this scenario," I told students. "This time, instead of just writing down what you imagine, also make some predictions of what the story will be about."

I wandered around the room and watched the students working. They were very much on task, staring dreamily into space or jotting down ideas. Tasha appeared at my elbow. "Mrs. Kissner," she said, "Where's the Grand Canyon?"

"Arizona," I answered reflexively.

"Hm," Tasha said, and returned to her seat. I stared after her for a moment, wondering where this question had come from.

Jose called me over to the other side of the room. "Can a ship sail up a canyon?" he asked. "I mean, what is a canyon anyway?"

I wondered if I should demonstrate what a canyon looks like. But then I started to wonder. How did Jose's question relate to the task? And why was it so similar to Tasha's question?

"Jose," I said, "How about if you read the words for me out loud?"

"Okay. Saltwater, wooden ship, canyons . . ." His face lit up. "Oh! It's not *canyons*, it's *cannons*!" He laughed. "That makes a lot more sense. I was trying to imagine a big ship going up a canyon."

Here is an example of how problems at the micro level can seriously impact deeper processing. Because they had misread a word, both Tasha and Jose were generating seriously flawed mental images. There was some self-monitoring going on, however. Both students had an intuitive sense that something was wrong, which caused them to ask me questions in an attempt to get more information. This entire episode shows the power of mental imagery, as the strange picture that they concocted was a signal to these students that something had gone wrong with their reading.

I asked them if they would be comfortable with me talking about what had happened. "This isn't a mistake to feel bad about," I told them. "What you did was really cool. You had a picture in your mind that just didn't feel right, and you looked for more information to resolve this problem. That's just what I want you to be doing!"

Smiling sheepishly, Tasha stood in front of the class and explained what she had done. "So I was picturing this big ship going through a canyon, but I didn't think there are canyons near saltwater. But then Mrs. Kissner had me read the words again, and I realized that the word was *cannons*. And then I started thinking about pirates."

Other students in the class were nodding. On the papers that I had read, the word *pirates* appeared again and again. The recent pirate movies had built a strong schema for ships with cannons, and the students started talking about images of battles, stowaways, and bloodthirsty pirates.

In the third scenario, I wanted to show students how they can refine their schema with the addition of new information. The words were *scientist, expedition, rain forest, beetle*. Here, students began with a very broad schema and slowly narrowed down their images. Patrick wrote, "A scientist discovers a new species of beetles." Through his mental images, Patrick was able to call up words like *species*. Shannon said, "It sounds like what I want to do, only I want to research frogs." With this scenario, students added words or events they expect in the story.

For the fourth and final scenario, I wanted to show students that their mental images needed to change as new information arrives. The first three words that I showed them were *classroom, students, teachers*. As I expected, students wrote about the usual classroom scene. Samantha wrote, "I imagine Mrs. Kissner teaching the class."

But when I read the last two list entries, *slates* and *one room*, students exclaimed aloud. Later, they talked about how their visualizations had changed. "I was picturing just an ordinary classroom, but then I thought about a one-room schoolhouse," Bria said.

"I pictured where we went on our field trip last year, the Mud College," Abigail put in.

"It's weird. At first I was picturing kids and teachers like from today, but then that all changed in my mind and I was picturing them wearing, you know, old-fashioned clothes," Brendan said.

By learning about how to activate their schemas, students were well on their way to building strong mental images. To adapt this to your own classroom, you can alter the key words for each scenario, adding or subtracting until the words match upcoming lessons or stories. In subsequent guided reading lessons, we continued talking about how we could use our schemas to help us visualize a scene. Students even began to see the activity as a sort of game and asked me to give them words to visualize in the odd moments before lunch.

But visualization is not only about details from our schema. Students must also become sensitive to the text details, the small clues that the author is sharing. This was our next step.

Visualizing with Struggling Readers

Activating a schema can be dangerous. Sometimes, students stick too closely to their initial expectations of a text, failing to update their mental images with new information.

Carl Hiaasen's book *Hoot* features a very nasty, very rotten bully by the name of Dana Matherson (Hiaasen 2002). After reading about Dana on the first few pages of the book, I asked students to tell me how they pictured the character.

"I think she looks really really mean," Andrea said.

"She?" I asked.

"Yeah. Dana's a girl's name, right?"

In the text, Dana is actually a boy and is referred to by masculine pronouns. But for some reason, this hadn't registered with Andrea. She had operated from her understanding that Dana is a girl's name and had not taken into account new information from the text.

In the Setting Schema activity's fourth scenario, when students knew that they were supposed to change their mental images, they were able to do so. In natural reading situations, however, a mental switch does not always happen so easily. Many students have trouble with flexibly changing and refining their images. Their mental pictures firmly refuse to budge, even in the face of contradictory details. Not surprisingly, the students who have the most trouble with altering their mental images are also the students who have trouble with overall reading comprehension.

I design my instruction with two distinct plans in mind. First, struggling readers need to know how to ground their visualization in text details. They need help in recognizing how to pull certain details out of a text and use them to justify a mental image. In addition, these students need experience with stories that offer a payoff for visualizing. To help them internalize the visualizing process, students need to read stories with strong appeal.

Grounding Visualizations in Text Details

A reader needs to constantly return to the text for details to refine a sensory image. As in the example from *Hoot*, though, sometimes struggling readers are not sensitive to the details in text that can lead them to different mental images. In addition, sometimes they pull from background knowledge that is inappropriate for the text. I'll never forget when I was teaching a series of night poems. These poems were rich in imagery of stars, planets, and nighttime animals. I started the lesson by having students brainstorm images that came to mind when they thought of *night*. I imagined talking about fireflies, campfires, camping, and owls. I certainly did not expect the responses students gave me, filled with references to slasher films and horror villains. The students did have quite a schema for *night*. Unfortunately, the ideas that they had activated would not lead them to deep processing of the text.

Students needed to be shown how to refine their thinking. With the night poems, I handed students the page of poems, complete with illustrations of stars and peaceful hillsides. "Is there anything here that might lead you to think of horror movies?" I asked students, keeping my voice neutral. When they admitted that no, the page did not lead them to think about violent themes, I said, "Making predictions about a text and activating your schemas are great. You need to remember to look back to the text, though. Because there's nothing here related to gory movies, you will need to push those thoughts aside." I acted this out, and some students copied my gesture. "Push aside those thoughts, and get your schemas going in the direction of the text."

Afterward, Brad asked, "Can you add stuff to your schema?"

"Of course," I said.

"Because I really liked the last poem, the one about the stars. I think I'm going to add that to my schema of *night*."

Students were on the right track. They knew that they needed to access prior knowledge before reading, but they also needed more experience at paying attention to the details in the text. Some carefully structured activities were needed to help students see how they need to keep text details in mind as they visualize. This activity also led students to see how they can pull specific details from a text to support their ideas. I designed the Visualizing: Using Details from the Text activity (Figure 7–2) as a very clear, very explicit way to do this.

This is a fairly easy activity. Students read a short passage, and then they identify which of two pictures matches the monster. Then, they need to identify the text details that helped them to make their choice. The purpose of this is to get students matching key text details with key features in a picture.

The second passage is a little trickier. The title, "The New Ship," causes students to activate their schemas for *ship*. Many students imagine a tall boat under sail. However, the details in the passage clearly show that this ship is not a watercraft, but a spaceship. This is just another way for students to experience a shift in their mental images. As we discussed it, students were able to pinpoint the exact place in the passage where their visualization changed. They felt successful and confident in their new abilities. When Lindsay wrote in her reading journal that week, she pulled a specific detail from the text to support her ideas. "This book is really neat. It has lots of neat details, like blue gleaming fire. I could really picture that."

A Payoff for Visualizing

I learned to be very cautious when planning lessons for these struggling readers. Many of the books written for below-grade-level readers look nice and glossy, but have rather dull, painful text. Often, the description is just tacked on to the story, with little relation to what is really going on. But this is just the opposite of what I want for these students. They need to feel pulled in by a story, need to understand how visualizing leads to a fuller understanding of what is going on. Stories need to include some payoff for visualizing.

I decided to write a story for one of my reading groups. Because I wanted to focus on sensory images, I decided to include as many strong details as I could. Pulling from a wealth of experience with cleaning my room as a child, I wrote the story "Cleaning Up" (Figure 7–3).

As I read this story with a group of struggling readers, we started by activating our schemas about cleaning up. Students were eager to share stories of how they cleaned—or didn't clean—their rooms. Then, we talked about how so much of the story depends upon what the reader is imagining. The story lives in the text details. If the students don't have

Visualizing: Using Details from the Text

Good readers visualize. They make pictures in their minds as they read. Today, you will learn about using text details to help you make accurate pictures.

Matt and the Monster

Matt stared at the huge monster. It was covered in shaggy fur. The monster's face had only one eye, but it had two long curved horns. Below the upturned nose, a wide mouth grinned. "Trick or treat!" the monster said.

Directions: Look at the pictures. Which one shows the monster? Underline the text details that support your choice.

The New Ship

"She's a beauty," the captain said. He was admiring his new ship.

"Yes," agreed the first mate. He ran his hand over the smooth white sides of the ship. He opened the door and stepped inside. A sleek control panel was in front of him. A glass window showed the darkness of distant space.

"We'll be able to travel far in this ship," said the captain. He looked out the window. "We'll see many new planets."

Directions: Look at the pictures. Which one shows the new ship? Underline the text details that support your choice.

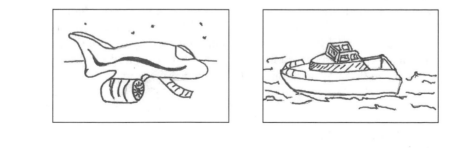

Figure 7–2.

Cleaning Up

Mark tried to walk through his little brother's room. First he tripped over a pile of dirty clothes in the middle of the floor. As he fell, he grabbed onto the desk. The desk was covered with tiny Lego pieces and old cookies. Mark's hand was covered in goo.

"Yuck," said Mark. When he took another step, he slipped on a Matchbox car. He slid across the room. He passed a castle made out of blocks. He fell into a pile of comic books and apple cores.

"Joey!" said Mark.

Joey came into the room. "Yeah?"

"I'm in charge while Mom and Dad are at work," Mark said. "I say you need to clean up this mess. And do it right!"

Joey looked around the room. "Okay," he said.

Mark went into his room and started his homework. He could hear Joey working next door. "Good," he thought. "That room is a disaster."

Soon, Joey came and knocked on Mark's door. Mark wasn't even finished his math homework yet. "I'm done," said Joey.

Mark didn't believe it. "How could you be finished already?" he asked.

"Come and see," said Joey.

Mark walked over to Joey's room. He looked at the floor. "The floor looks clean," said Mark.

Mark checked out Joey's desk. "The desk looks clean," he said.

The pile of comic books and apple cores was gone. There were no Matchbox cars to be seen anywhere. The Legos and the old cookies were all gone too.

Mark looked under the bed. It was clean. He opened up a dresser drawer. There was nothing inside. "I don't know how you did it," Mark said. "Your whole room is clean."

"I know," said Joey.

Mark had an idea. "Let's go out and play some football to celebrate," he said. "Get your coat."

Joey stood in front of the closet door. He looked nervous. "It's warm out," he said.

"No, it's not," said Mark. "I'm in charge, and I say you need your coat. Come on. Football will be fun."

Joey didn't move. Mark pushed past him and opened the closet door.

Whoosh! Out came the apple cores and comic books. Out came the piles of clothing. Out came the Legos, the old cookies, the blocks, plus a whole bunch of other things.

"Well," said Mark, who was buried underneath all of the junk. "I think I've figured out how you cleaned your room."

FIGURE 7–3.

the mental picture of the contents of the closet pouring out, they will not understand how Joey cleaned the room. I intentionally wrote the story so that it would present very few decoding problems. I wanted students to be able to concentrate on visualizing instead of decoding.

Another interesting book for helping readers of all abilities focus on visualizing is *Trouble on the Tracks*. This picture book by Kathy Mallat leads the reader into believing that the story is about a regular train (Mallat 2001). Toward the end of the book, the details become rather odd. The author casually mentions that the train comes off the tracks—an accident that seems a little too disturbing for the way it is described. As it turns out, the book is about a toy train set, and "Trouble" is the name of the young engineer's cat. When I presented it to students, I did not show them the pictures. Instead, I had them draw what they were imagining at different points in the story. When we reached the point where the story changed, they were able to talk about the details that led them to a new understanding of the story. Through the Setting Schema and Visualizing: Using Details from the Text activities, students built a foundation for this change of sensory image. Students were able to draw on what they had already learned to deal with the new text.

Conclusion

Our ability to visualize is amazing. Readers can pull on schema to build mental images, filling in gaps in information with details from their memory. When students learn about visualizing, they are often surprised at how individual words and phrases can trigger their schemas. However, students must also learn how to ground their mental images in the text and avoid being pulled from the author's words by the pictures in their minds. Readers also benefit from seeing stories that have a payoff for visualizing or stories in which some of the action must be imagined.

What to Teach About Details and Visualizing

- Visualizing depends on the reader's schema, as authors never give all of the details in a scene.

- Teaching students how to use words to activate their schemas can help them be more aware of details in the text.

- Struggling readers often fail to notice the text details that would cause them to change their mental images.

- Stories that depend on a visual image for humor or meaning can help readers see a payoff for visualizing.

8 USING DETAILS TO UNDERSTAND GENRE

As every teacher knows, maintaining a classroom library is a hard task. There are always issues of how to organize the books, how to keep track of who has which book, and how to make sure that books are returned.

In the last several years, though, there has been one section of my library that is always in order. My historical fiction section, which takes up two shelves, is usually neat and tidy, an island of order in the midst of chaos. Why? It's not that my students take extra special care of these books. In fact, the opposite is true. I can rarely ever convince students to read them.

And it's not for lack of trying. I love historical fiction and keep a current collection of the latest books. When students come to me for recommendations for an independent reading book, I usually give them a selection of three books, tailored to their reading tastes and abilities. No matter how much I try to push historical fiction, it languishes on the shelves. I read *A Long Way from Chicago* as a read-aloud to help students learn how to deal with the genre (Peck 1998). They were excited when I told them that there was a sequel. "Really? There's another one?" Matt asked.

I pulled it from the shelf, ready to put it in his waiting hands. But he said, "Could you do that for the next read-aloud? I don't really like historical fiction, but it's okay when you read it."

By sixth grade, many students do have pronounced reading preferences. There are genres they like and genres they avoid. When I investigated why students preferred certain genres, I learned that details play an important role in determining what students like to read. I also learned that when students start to avoid a genre, they're likely to continue avoiding it.

How Genres Shape Reading Experiences

In this chapter, we'll look at the fiction and nonfiction genres that students most often study in school. This chapter is not meant to be a discussion of characteristics of different genres and how to teach them. Instead, we will focus on how details affect the understanding of genre and how genre determines the details that are deemed important by the reader.

At its most basic, text can be divided into drama, poetry, and prose. The category of prose can be further divided into nonfiction, the domain of true information, and fiction, the land of make-believe. Students sometimes try to simplify this to "true" and "not true," but I try to steer them away from these terms. Fiction is not untrue; it exists in a totally different universe, a microworld created by the author, a world in which the rules of true and not true might be completely upended.

People do sometimes try to treat genres as this black-and-white concept; as a beginning teacher, I remember looking through books, trying to find a list of the "right" genres. There is no such list. Stories exist before they are categorized into genres, and different people categorize stories in different ways. Here are the genres I've found most useful to discuss in the classroom:

- mystery

- realistic fiction

- science fiction

- fantasy

- historical fiction

- folklore

- biography

- informational

Each of these genres may be further subdivided. Within the realm of realistic fiction, for instance, there are sports stories, humor, and adventure stories. Stories with talking animals could be considered to fit in the fantasy genre, and folklore includes fables, legends, and tall tales. And then there are increasing numbers of stories that blend elements of multiple genres, as well as newly emerging genres like the verse-novel (Alexander 2005).

Ice cream is a useful metaphor for understanding genres. When you go into a new ice cream shop and order a vanilla ice cream cone, you know what to expect. Even though ice cream may vary slightly in flavor and texture, all vanilla ice cream shares some characteristics. Genres are the same way. Different books in the fantasy genre may vary in characters and setting, but they all have some common flavors.

Remember, readers represent meaning through the surface level, textbase, and situation model. How readers form this representation is influenced by the readers' understanding of the features, components, and ground rules of the genre (Graesser, Millis, and Zwaan 1997). In other words, readers draw on their knowledge of a genre to help them build meaning from the text.

At the surface level, a reader of fantasy will have knowledge of words for different magical creatures. The general structure of a story will help a reader construct a coherent textbase by linking events. And prior knowledge about the genre will cause a reader to build a rich situation model, making elaborative inferences about characters and their goals, traits, and emotions.

Each genre has its own set of rules. When I start a fantasy, I know that I will encounter something magical or mysterious in the early pages. I also know that every author uses different rules of magic and that the magic of a book by Diana Wynne Jones will be slightly different than the magic of a book by Tamora Pierce. One of my tasks as a reader, then, is to figure out how magic works in each book's universe.

Readers use the rules of a genre to build inferences about the story. Suppose that you were reading this paragraph on the second page of a book.

> "What was that sound?" Mia asked.
> "I don't know," her brother answered uneasily. "It sounded like it came from the attic."

If you knew from the cover of the book that this was a realistic fiction, then you would make a very different prediction about the nature of the sound than if it were a fantasy. For skilled readers, this process happens almost automatically. Information from the front cover of a book, knowledge of the author, and even clues from the author's style can lead a reader to make sophisticated inferences that draw on a wealth of background knowledge.

Details in Different Genres

But how do readers determine the genre of a particular book or novel? The differences between genres can be found at both the level of individual words and sentences, or the micro level, and the level of the overall text, or the macro level.

At the micro level, genres will pull from different sets of words. The words *hoop skirt* might bring to mind a historical fiction, and *interplanetary protection gear* sounds like science fiction. A "clue" is very important to mystery, while "riding a bus to school" is an event that would be expected in realistic fiction. As I started to write this chapter, I considered creating two very similar stories of different genres. Only the small details would be different—for instance, in the science fiction version of the story, the mother might ask the girl to program a robot to clean up the room; in the historical fiction story, the girl might have the chore of carrying water from the well.

Intriguing as this seemed, I cast aside the idea. Although there are many differences between genres at the micro level, the true nature of a genre can only be understood at the level of the whole text, or the macro level. Of course there will be micro-level differences between historical fiction and science fiction. But the more important differences are the differences in conflict, setting, and theme—all macro-level constructs. Historical fiction often involves a conflict that stems from the historical time period. The setting does not exist as a simple backdrop but is an integral part of the story. Science fiction often explores the interaction of humans and technology at the very boundaries of science. To say that these genres are only different because of some surface details at the micro level would be misleading.

But this brings us back to the original question. How do readers determine the genre of a book? To pull on rich background knowledge about the characteristics of the genre, a reader needs to figure out the genre in the first few pages of the book. In real-life reading situations, this isn't a problem. The genre is usually easily apparent from a cover. It makes sense that publishers know how to market a book to entice likely readers. Think about the covers to the Harry Potter series. With their foil lettering and stylized pictures, they are obviously fantasy. Students know that books with pictures of magical creatures will usually turn out to be fantasy, just as books with old-fashioned pictures will be historical fiction and books with aliens will be science fiction. Problem solved.

Well, not really. Looking at the cover to a book is a great strategy for independent reading time. But what about on standardized tests, when students do not have access to pictures or fancy titles? This is a situation that can lead kids into trouble. After all, it's known that less skilled readers have trouble finding the important information that is conveyed in the title and the exposition of a story (Perfetti, Landi, and Oakhill 2005). Without knowing the genre of a story, these readers will fail to access the appropriate prior knowledge. They will not have the rich, deep processing that leads to strong comprehension.

For this reason, students need to be taught how to sample a few details at the micro level to help them figure out the genre. Once they know the genre of the story, they can use the details to build a more global understanding.

Teaching Students How to Use Details to Figure Out Genre
Before students can independently find the genres of different stories, they need to have an awareness of different fiction genres. I start discussing genre when I offer independent reading books on the first day of school. As the days go by, students sign in for morning meeting by matching books they've read to genres; we make lists of genres that students have read; and we even match popular movies and television shows to their genres. Throughout the year, I always include genre as we discuss stories and books.

Once students have a basic understanding of genre, they're ready to begin figuring out the genres of different stories. I started the lesson by comparing the reading experience with landing on an unknown planet. "Once your spaceship touches down and you get out, you need to figure out very quickly what you're dealing with. What's important? What's dangerous? How will you survive? It's the same way when you're reading a story. You need to figure out very quickly who the main characters are, what the setting is, and what the genre is. This will help you understand the rest of the story."

To help students see the connection between visualizing and determining a genre, I revisited the Setting Schema activity from Chapter 7. This time, students used the words to visualize the scene and figure out what the genre of the story might be. With sets of words like *ogre, unicorn, book, amulet* and *party, rumors, argument, friendship*, I was able to test the depth of my students' genre knowledge. Collections of words like *summer, camping, missing tent, flashlight* helped us look at where the boundaries of the different genres overlap. The last four words might point to realistic fiction, or they might indicate mystery. In this case, the reader would need to do some more reading before making a final determination of genre. I asked students to generate some words that would clearly show the story to be a mystery. When they came up with *clue* and *detective*, I knew that they were able to bring their background knowledge to the task.

Next, I showed the students some short excerpts and modeled looking for details to determine genre. This activity, What's the Genre? (Figure 8–1), allowed me to show students what details were most important to figuring out a genre.

Decoding problems can cause students some trouble. I've noticed that students who have trouble decoding often just skip over longer words. You can probably guess which word from excerpt #1 my struggling readers skipped over—*Confederate*. But this word is one of the clearest clues that this is historical fiction. This is an example of how decoding problems can lead to deeper issues with comprehension. A struggling reader doesn't recognize that this story takes place during the Civil War. The reader fails to activate relevant schemas related to the Civil War and then misses out on future references to the conflict. As historical information is conveyed in the text, the reader won't integrate new information about the Civil War into existing schemas. A problem with one word can have far-reaching effects. (Just as a note, my students should have fairly well-developed knowledge of the Civil War—most drive through sections of the Gettysburg battlefield just to go shopping. I wrote excerpt #1 based on a newspaper article about how the nearby city of York surrendered to the Confederates in the days leading up to the fateful battle. Using bits and pieces from your area's local history can make the genre of historical fiction somewhat more tangible for students.)

Excerpt #2 is clearly realistic fiction. Details like the transfer bus, school building, and the conversation with the aide show this. Students will sometimes say that realistic fiction "doesn't have a genre." Because realistic fiction operates under the same rules as the here and now, the details of realistic fiction just slide right by. These students seem to have assimilated genre into their schema for *other*—a genre is something that is beyond the real world. Interestingly, these are often the same students who tell me quite earnestly that they don't have a culture. But understanding the conventions of realistic fiction is still very important. For example, the conflict in realistic fiction often stems from friendship or school issues, both of which are seen in this excerpt.

After students have seen me model how to find genre, they are ready for a more rigorous activity. I photocopy the first pages of several different books and give them to groups of students. Working cooperatively, the groups read the pages and try to identify the genre of the book. A benefit of cooperative groups is that background knowledge can become shared. Students can learn from the reading experiences of all the students in their group and see how the different genres can be explained and represented differently (Nuthall 1999b).

As we work on test preparation activities in guided reading groups, I often start a new text by having students scan and make some guesses about the genre. The more experience students have, the more likely they are to be able to pull on this genre knowledge every time they encounter new text. After we finish the story, going back to our predictions about the genre will help students to see how genres compare at the macro level.

A running list of books and stories that the class has read is a handy resource for these discussions. I use a side wall of my classroom to show off texts we've shared as described in *Guiding Readers and Writers* (Fountas and Pinnell 2001). Megan McLean, who teaches next door, showed me a neat twist that includes students in making the list. After we read a story, I write the title on a sheet of paper. Students then volunteer to decorate the titles. By the end of the year, the student-decorated chain of texts we've shared wraps around the room.

A list of texts can help discussions about genre become more specific. In April, when we read *The Field Guide*, the first book in The Spiderwick Chronicles, some students thought that it was realistic fiction (DiTerlizzi and Black 2003). "I mean, Jared and Simon are real, and they go to school, just like in *There's a Boy in the Girls' Bathroom*," said Lindsay, pointing to the list of texts on the wall (Sachar 1987). "That was realistic fiction, right? So I think this is realistic fiction too."

"What are some differences between the two books?" I asked. Several other students offered comments about the magical creatures in Spiderwick, and how the conflict in the first book was resolved by turning a boggart into a brownie.

"I mean, look," Shannon said, picking up the copy of the book that she had bought on her own. "Look at these pictures. Is that realistic? I mean, if the story just had Jared and Simon getting in trouble, that would be realistic fiction. But I think it's fantasy."

What's the Genre?

Knowing the genre of a story helps a reader understand what is going on.

Directions: Can you figure out the genre of the story excerpts? Circle the genre below. Underline the details that help you decide on the genre.

Historical fiction	Realistic fiction	Science fiction/ fantasy	Mystery

Excerpt #1

I sighed. Nothing had been the same since this war had started. But last year, it was comforting to think that the fighting was far away, in Virginia and other places that I didn't bother to learn about in geography. This spring, though, things were different. The Confederate army had come north, into Pennsylvania. And now they were about to march through our own town. "Do you think they'll cause any trouble?" I asked.

Meg shrugged. "They said they wouldn't. We'll see what happens."

"Where are they going?" I asked. Even though I was older than Meg, I took it for granted that she knew more about the war than I did. She was thirteen and nosy. I don't just mean that she would listen in on conversations when she heard her name. No, Meg took nosiness to a whole new level. She would creep around outside closed doors, putting her ear up to the keyhole in the hopes of hearing good gossip. She could stand still as a post for an entire hour, making people forget she was around, so they would loosen their tongues and spill all the news.

"The river, of course," she said. "They probably want to get across to Lancaster or Harrisburg."

Genre: _____

Details that helped me figure out the genre: _____

_____

_____

_____

Questions that I might expect to find answered as I read: _____

_____

_____

_____

FIGURE 8–1.

Historical fiction	Realistic fiction	Science fiction/ fantasy	Mystery

Excerpt #2

Michael's head bumped against the cold glass of the window as the school bus went through a deep pothole. He sighed and readjusted his glasses. He shouldn't have to feel so nervous. It wasn't fair to have two first days of school in one year. But here he was, at the beginning of the second week of school, facing a new teacher, new class, new kids, new building.

Nothing about the situation was fair. Instead of one bus ride, now he had two. First he had to get on his regular bus, the one that he had ridden since kindergarten, and ride to his old familiar school building. He had to get off that bus with everyone else. But instead of going into the familiar hallways, he got turned aside by the aide on the sidewalk.

"You! Aren't you riding the transfer bus?" she asked, waving a pink slip of paper.

"Yeah. But I was going to go in and say good-bye to my friend—"

"You can't go in. You have to get on the transfer bus right now," she insisted.

So he hadn't even been allowed to go in and tell Taylor, who had been his friend since they both fell off the merry-go-round in kindergarten, about the phone call last Friday afternoon, about the hushed conversations of his parents, or the final decision that he, Michael, was to go to Indian's Mark Elementary School from now on.

Genre: _____

Details that helped me to figure out the genre: _____

_____

_____

_____

_____

Questions that I might expect to find answered as I read: _____

_____

_____

_____

_____

_____

FIGURE 8–1. *continued*

Lindsay admitted that the pictures were not realistic. "So it's fantasy?" she asked, digesting the idea. I knew from her reading logs of the year that she had stuck with mostly realistic fiction and mysteries. Our class discussion was helping her build a schema for the characteristics of fantasy. Having easy access to a list of books that we had already read added a new dimension to our discussion.

Why Students May Dislike Certain Genres

If students understand different genres and can identify the genre of stories, why are there some genres that they just don't like? When I asked students, their answers all sounded similar.

"It just doesn't interest me."

"I don't like all the details."

"It's boring."

What determines interesting text, then? There are many possible explanations, but two ideas have proven to be very useful to my classroom: getting the right blend of new details and old information and taking details away from a text versus living in the text.

Getting the Right Blend of New Details and Old Information

For many readers, it all seems to come down to schema. People are drawn to tasks and texts that are moderately familiar (Yarlas 1999). That is, readers will enjoy a text that has a familiar feel but is not overly repetitive. This explains the allure of the series books that fill our bookshelves. When students read books in a series, they encounter slightly different stories with the same characters and settings, creating the moderate familiarity that is appealing to students. For less skilled readers, series books may be an especially important way to help fill in gaps in genre knowledge. Each book in a series will highlight the characteristics of that genre.

The knowledge-schema theory of interest may also explain why readers are drawn to certain genres. According to this idea, people are interested in information that leads them to modify or enhance their existing schema (Yarlas 1999). Although this theory was created to explain interest in expository text, I think it could apply to fiction as well. I recently read *Red Moon at Sharpsburg* by Rosemary Wells (2007). I had some knowledge of the Civil War battle from driving through the town and canoeing on the Antietam Creek. In the course of reading the book, however, I learned new details that caused me to change my schema for the battle. Modification of schema is supposed to lead to interest. In my case, I was drawn into the book by my desire to add to my prior knowledge. A moderate level of familiarity led to a high level of interest.

When students have no schema for a topic, they are unlikely to find it interesting. This leads to a negative feedback loop for genre knowledge.

Students don't know about a genre, so they don't find it interesting; they don't read books in that genre, so they don't build their knowledge.

I think that the genre of historical fiction faces even more of a challenge, because students have few schemas for historical events. Authors often assume that readers know about people and events, and they don't explain the setting clearly. Writers of science fiction and fantasy, on the other hand, know that readers will be unfamiliar with the settings of their books. They compensate by adding more clear detail to entice the reader to stick with the book. J. K. Rowling, the successful author of the Harry Potter series, knew that her readers would have no prior knowledge of Quidditch. She built the schema for the wizard game by revealing details throughout the books. By now, many young readers probably know more about Quidditch than the Civil War.

Taking Details Away from a Text Versus Living in the Text

In any classroom, it quickly becomes apparent that students approach the classroom library with very different agendas. There are some students who pore over nonfiction texts, writing down details and even making charts in their reading response journals. And then there are other readers who will disappear under a table for the entire reading time, lost in the world of fantasy. These readers have different expectations for their reading.

Reading with the purpose to take away information and facts is *efferent* reading. This is the kind of reading used to attack nonfiction books, instructions, journal articles, and even this book. Efferent reading requires close concentration, attention to details, and the ability to take away important ideas that will be used later (Rosenblatt 1988).

At the other end of the spectrum is *aesthetic* reading. Reading for an aesthetic purpose is reading for the experience, the feeling of being transported by the text. Sometimes a reader can be so drawn in by the emotions of a text that they fail to recall key details.

How do these modes of reading interact in a classroom? Although readers can shift between the different modes, some have marked preferences. Stacy was an example of a student who preferred aesthetic reading. She was closely attuned to how what she read made her feel. Her favorite books from the school year included poetry, coming-of-age novels, and books with a high emotional content. She was bored by texts that did not evoke an emotional response.

James, on the other hand, was more of an efferent reader. It's no wonder that he had little patience for discussing how books made him feel. He wanted texts that he could use. When given a choice, he grabbed the nonfiction books, and he brought his own hunting magazines to school. When I pressed him to read a novel, he chose *The Edge Chronicles*—an illustrated, detailed fantasy series (Stewart and Riddell 2004). Several of the other boys in the class chose the same series. The impromptu book discussions they held during morning homeroom centered on the map of the fantasy world and how all of the characters in the different books interconnected. They didn't waste time talking about the emotional journeys of the characters; they were more interested in poring over the maps and tracing the physical routes the characters traversed.

Aesthetic and Efferent Readers in the Classroom

Have you ever had a conference with a child who swore that she finished a book but could not answer the simplest literal questions? It's easy to assume that the child is lying and didn't actually read the book. But sometimes the case is not so simple. Consider what happened when I read *The Lightning Thief*, a book about a young boy who discovers that he is a half-blood, the son of one of the gods of Olympus. In the course of the book, Percy undertakes a quest to the Underworld, aided by two loyal friends and a magic sword named Riptide (Riordan 2005).

A few months later, my husband and son started listening to the book on CD. They had heard my descriptions and were hooked. "When does Percy get the magic sword?" my son Zachary asked.

I thought about it. "Um, I think it's a gift from his father. At the end," I replied, although I wasn't at all sure. A few more chapters of listening proved my error. Percy received the sword fairly early in the book. Without the sword, he could never have succeeded on his quest and would have been killed by monsters.

"Did you really read this book?" my husband asked, with mock sternness. At first the question made me feel offended. Of course I had read the book! I had felt Percy's embarrassment at his dyslexia and ADHD; understood his disappointment at his father's lack of interest in his life; shared his grief in the disappearance of his mother. I had lived the adventures of Percy Jackson. And yet I could not remember when he had received his sword.

As you can probably tell, I tend to fall back into the aesthetic mode when I read for enjoyment. Once I knew that I would be talking about *The Lightning Thief* with other readers—specifically, my husband and my son—I went back to the text with the goal of retaining more details. Sharing a discussion caused me to switch gears and change from simply experiencing the text to trying to bring information away from the text.

Realizing my own preferences has helped me guide reading discussions and judge student comprehension in the classroom. Based on a student's preferred style of reading, I can make some guesses about where the child will excel and where she will need more support. For example, I know that students like Stacy will need help with finding the details to support her creative, intuitive ideas. Tasks like science reading and directions are slightly more difficult, as they require these readers to shift out of a comfort zone and into a more efferent reading style.

Students like James, on the other hand, will enjoy reading directions and dealing with practical applications for reading. These students may have trouble with making inferences about characters' emotions and may initially resist reading texts without an apparent purpose, like poetry.

Of course, I don't make these judgments overnight. Just because a student reads one book of nonfiction, for example, does not mean that the student only wants to partake of efferent reading. From the beginning of the year, I use a clipboard to keep track of the books that students read. Double-entry response journals, in which students summarize what they read and write their reactions to their reading, provide me with more information.

To help me learn even more, I developed a survey. What Kind of Reader Are You? (Figure 8–2) is a way to show students how their reading preferences can affect their understanding of text. I had noticed that my students, especially the girls, loved to complete surveys. I harnessed that enthusiasm into a survey that asks students to choose between a series of books and statements.

As they completed the surveys and interpreted the results, many seemed surprised. "It's as if they're describing everything about me!" Shannon exclaimed. Maggie also agreed with the results of the survey. As she wrote on her reflection, "I agreed with my reading style, I like to enjoy reading books, and I'm not a big fan of nonfiction." When she reflected on what she could do to become a better reader, she wrote, "I need to think about reading more nonfiction, and about how I can use the information I read."

I emphasized to students that the most important part of this survey was the process of considering their reading preferences. At the end of the day, it doesn't matter terribly whether students are efferent or aesthetic readers. What does matter is that they are aware of their preferences, and know how those preferences can be assets or liabilities in their reading.

Building Genre Knowledge

How do we help students build their genre knowledge? Reading aloud is an excellent answer. When I choose books, I look first to the genres that students neglect. When students aren't reading good books of a certain genre, it's a clear message to me that they don't find that genre interesting. I can change this by building their background knowledge and showing them the important elements of the genre.

In guided reading, I choose to use many short texts instead of reading novels. This is hard, because it feels as if I am always looking for the next story. But when we read a new story every few days, students can try little tidbits of different genres. Maybe a whole book of science fiction is not appealing. A short story, read with a small group, can be a less overwhelming introduction to the genre. *Cricket* magazine is a good source of short stories for young readers and features stories in a variety of genres.

What Kind of Reader Are You?

As you progress as a reader, it's important to think about your reading preferences. Here is a short survey for you to complete and score.

Part 1

Directions: You are in a library. Your job is to pick out three books for yourself. At every shelf, you have only two choices. Circle your choice.

Shelf 1	Book Titles
A	**True Facts About the World** This book is filled with pictures and text with real facts and information about the world.
B	**Difficult Decisions** This is a nonfiction book about boys and girls who have faced hard choices. In this book, you will learn about how the boys and girls felt and how they made their decisions.

Shelf 2	Book Titles
B	**Poems About Nature** This book has poems about the natural world. There are three sections: seasons, plants, and animals. Each poem is illustrated.
A	**A Field Guide to the Forest** This book tells about the plants and animals of the forest. You will see pictures of different animals, along with descriptions of what they eat and where they live. There are also pictures and descriptions of plants.

Shelf 3	Book Titles
A	**Pet Care** This book explains how to take care of different kinds of pets. It tells the reader what to feed pets, how to make sure they stay healthy, and how to train them.
B	**Pet Problems** This book is about the friendship between a girl and her dog. Although her mother does not want the girl to have a dog, she adopts a stray and learns how to take care of it.

FIGURE 8–2.

Part 2

Directions: What would you prefer? For each choice, circle one box.

B	I would rather read a book that showed me how people in different places deal with problems and challenges.
A	I would rather read a book that taught me how to do something.

B	I sometimes skip ahead in books to get to good parts.
A	I like to know all the details of a book, so I don't skip.

B	Sometimes I feel as if I read "way down deep" in a book, and really experience the events.
A	When books focus too much on feelings, I have trouble getting interested.

B	I like reading poetry, even poems I don't understand right away.
A	Why can't authors just say exactly what they mean?

A	After I read a story, I remember specific details about the setting and characters.
B	After I read a story, I remember the big ideas from the story, such as the theme and the mood.

A	I'd rather read a complicated mystery book.
B	I'd rather read a book about relationships.

A	I like to think about ideas from my reading even after I have finished the book.
B	I prefer to think about ideas from the book while I am totally engaged in reading.

FIGURE 8–2. *continued*

Part 3: What This Means

Readers have different styles of reading. Some readers like to read to learn new things and gather details. These readers use a style of reading called *efferent* reading. *Efferent* reading is reading for the purpose of taking away information.

Some readers, on the other hand, like to experience a book or story as they read. These readers use a style of reading called *aesthetic* reading. *Aesthetic* reading is reading for the purpose of feeling ideas and emotions.

Scoring Your Responses

Look back at your responses. Each box has an "A" or "B." Mark the number of boxes that you checked with each letter.

A responses	
B responses	

If You Checked Mostly "A" Responses . . .	If You Checked Mostly "B" Responses . . .	If Your Answers Are Equally Divided . . .
You like to read for the purpose of getting information. You enjoy reading nonfiction, and you like to take away important details.	You like to read for feelings. You enjoy putting yourself in the place of the characters and imagining how you would feel. You can read so deeply that you feel as if the events in a story were actually happening to you.	You like a variety of reading materials. Not only do you enjoy reading nonfiction, but you enjoy fiction as well. You look for both details and main ideas as you read.
Strengths You are especially good at reading and following directions. You gather new information from everything that you read.	*Strengths* You enjoy poetry. Even if you don't understand everything in a story or poem, you can still figure out big ideas. You like to see how people act in different circumstances, and you enjoy reading about friendships and relationships.	*Strengths* You like reading in many different genres. You can find your way through complicated books and remember both main ideas and details.
Remember to: • Try reading different genres, not just nonfiction. You will probably enjoy mysteries or fantasy stories with complicated plots. • Make connections between yourself and characters in a story. • Look for the big picture in a story instead of just focusing on details.	*Remember to:* • Try reading nonfiction. You might enjoy biographies and autobiographies. Look for important details and information to remember. • Think about how you can use information from what you read. • Think about how details relate to the main ideas of what you read.	*Remember to:* • Keep reading many different kinds of books and stories. • Balance reading for interesting details and reading for main ideas. • Think about your purpose for reading before you start a new text.

FIGURE 8–2. *continued*

Part 4: Reader Survey Reflection

Directions: Now it's time to reflect on your reading preferences.

1. What did you think of the survey? Was it easy to complete, or did you have trouble with some of the choices? _____

    _____

    _____

    _____

    _____

    _____

2. Do you agree with the statements about your reading style? Why or why not?

    _____

    _____

    _____

    _____

    _____

3. Based on this survey, what can you do to become a better reader?

    _____

    _____

    _____

    _____

    _____

FIGURE 8–2. *continued*

Conclusion

Readers draw from their schemas to help them understand stories in different genres. Although the true nature of a genre is apparent at the macro level, sometimes readers will need to use micro-level details to figure out the genre of a text.

People are most interested in material with which they are moderately familiar. When students avoid certain genres, they never have the opportunity to build their schema for that genre, and it remains uninteresting. Classroom experiences with different genres, like read-aloud and guided reading, offer chances for students to become familiar with new genres.

Does repeated experience with different genres change student reading habits? At the end of the year, I handed Natalie a copy of the historical fiction *Midnight Rider* and told her that I thought she would like it (Harlow 2005). She studied the book dubiously but didn't say no. A few weeks later, she told me that she had finished the book. "That's tremendous!" I said. "How did you feel about reading it?"

"I didn't think I'd like this book because I usually don't like history books," Natalie said, "but this one is different. The author doesn't expect you to know everything, but explains things. That makes it easy to understand. Like I didn't know what smallpox was, but the author tells all about it in the prologue."

In the case of this book, a skilled author found a way to overcome readers' lack of schema. When Natalie knew the details behind the events in the book, she found a new world of interesting text. With the right instruction and the right books, we can help readers enjoy stories in genres they've never tried before.

What to Teach About Details in Genres

- Genres can be differentiated by details at the micro level, or individual words, and details at the macro level, or the overall structure.

- When readers have to determine the genre of a story, they need to use micro-level details.

- Readers use their schemas for genres to build predictions and make inferences.

- When readers avoid certain genres, they lose opportunities to build their schemas for those genres.

- Readers have the most interest in material that is moderately familiar.

- Readers also enjoy text that leads them to modify or enhance their existing schemas.

- Efferent readers read for the purpose of taking information away from a text and may have more trouble inferring character feelings or viewpoints.

- Aesthetic readers read for the experience of reading and may not remember important details.

9 DETAILS IN EXPOSITORY TEXT

One of the many problems with the current standardized testing craze is that we become focused on a student's responses instead of thinking about the student. When we boil everything down to a, b, c, or d, right or wrong, basic or proficient, we miss a world of detail about our individual students.

If I learn enough about students, patterns emerge. These patterns are far more interesting than how many questions a student got correct. Consider the case of Brendan. In a fall nonfiction unit, I wanted to focus on having students understand main ideas and details, a key concept for sixth grade and something that was sure to come up on the state tests. I planned to combine language arts instruction with a science unit on biomes, building a rich unit in which students would encounter the same ideas in many different ways. To build my guided reading groups for the next three weeks, I decided to give a pretest. I used a sample test passage from our state's public release tasks, combined the given questions with some questions focused on main ideas and details, and gave it to the students.

To my surprise, Brendan ended up with one of the lowest pretest scores, two correct out of ten. I was shocked by this, because Brendan is a bright, inquisitive student. When questions came up in class, he almost jumped out of his seat to go and search the Internet for answers. He could sift through scores of hits to find interesting information. When all of my classroom fish started dying in September, Brendan brought in his own water tests strips, showed me how to use them, and helped me fix the tank. He even brought in his own fish encyclopedia—I'd never known such a book existed—and showed me the different requirements of different fish. In other words, Brendan is a capable student, one who seems to be able to integrate information from a variety of sources and learn from text.

Brendan's pretest results had me doubting my reality. Was there a hidden problem? Perhaps his participation and friendly attitude were masking an underlying reading disability. Maybe my observations were wrong. Maybe I needed to revisit all of what I thought was true about the nature of success in reading.

You can see how one student's pretest scores led me to a pretty deep existential crisis. But then I went back and considered the evidence.

I thought about Brendan's strengths. I knew from his mother that he had several fish tanks at home and knew all that he needed to do to keep those fish healthy. Then it dawned on me—to be successful at all of these different tasks, he had to have a fine eye for detail. He loved the details. And why not? The details held the information of value. In the details, he could find the correct pH level for the tank, how to fix high ammonia, which kinds of fish bear live young, and which can exist in communities. In the details, he could find why music is important in the classroom and why it's not a good idea to dye fish. Brendan's reading preferences and life experiences had taught him how to extract information quickly and easily.

Unfortunately, his reading style caused him to miss out on main ideas. Knowing this helped me plan my instruction. Brendan didn't need the kinds of strategies that I planned to use with the other readers who had similar scores. Brendan wasn't a disengaged reader. He was very engaged! Instead, he needed to learn how to control his reading processes. He needed to learn how to avoid the lure of seductive details, how to use the details to find a main idea, and how to figure out the way that details fit into the structure of a text. Giving him lower-level text or trying to find a mysterious reading problem would not have been productive. This is why it's so important to know your students.

The Nature of Expository Text

Not surprisingly, Brendan was drawn to nonfiction. Expository text for students has come a long way in recent years, with glossy pictures, inviting text features, and lively writing. Once considered a chore, nonfiction is often cited as a favorite for middle- and upper-grade students, especially students who are "efferent" readers and like to read in order to take information away from the text (Rosenblatt 1988).

The task of understanding expository text is fundamentally different from understanding narrative text. Although narrative text is usually organized in chronological order, the same way that we experience the world, there are a number of common structures for expository text. These different structures can make expository text more difficult for the reader to understand, especially when the text is not coherent—that is, when one idea is not clearly connected to the rest (Geiger and Millis 2004).

As students get older, they are expected to learn from expository text. They are expected to be able to open a book, read it, and learn the information. This process is not as simple as it seems. In this chapter, we'll examine what it means to learn from text. Then, we'll look at how the task, the text, and the reader's prior knowledge interact.

Learning from Text

As I started the unit on biomes, I had some clear goals for what students needed to learn. These goals, provided for me by the state standards, required that students be able to list characteristics of a biome, compare and contrast different biomes, and identify adaptations in plants and animals. I decided to have groups of students study different biomes with the purpose of presenting their information to the rest of the class. Although I would do some general instruction in class, I wanted them to learn much of the information about their assigned biomes by reading text.

What happens when readers learn from text? Let's think about the next paragraph and related questions.

> Have you ever heard of the chaparral? Not many people know about this interesting biome. Located in California, Australia, parts of South America, and the Mediterranean, the chaparral has mild, rainy winters and hot, dry summers. Because of this, the landscape looks lush and green in the winter, but hot summers make everything dry and brown.

This is a pretty simple paragraph, one that is characteristic of many of the resources students used to learn about their biomes. Questions can help us see how a reader might represent the details of the paragraph.

"Where is the chaparral located?" This question elicits the reader's surface understanding of the text. An answer can be found by simply skimming the paragraph and looking for place names. Does this prove that the reader learned anything? Not really.

"What is the chaparral like?" This question can be answered through the reader's literal understanding of the text, or the textbase. Although it does require more thinking than the first question, it still does not prove that the reader actually learned anything from the text.

"How is the chaparral different from a desert?" When a question requires a reader-based inference, it requires the reader to activate schema and somehow integrate new information. For this question, the reader must open up the *desert* schema and think about a desert's characteristics. Then, the reader must use information from the text and compare the chaparral to the desert. Do they match? Probably not, as the chaparral seems to receive more rain. The reader then integrates the concept of chaparral into the existing *desert* schema—maybe by thinking, "chaparral—like desert, but not quite."

This is the essence of learning from text. A reader must be processing the text at all three levels: surface level, textbase, and situation model. A reader must activate an existing schema, and somehow add to or change that schema, integrating the new information into existing knowledge structures (Cote 1994). In this model, the details of a text become an important bridge between new information and old. The detail of the chaparral's rainy season is what keeps it from being a desert. This detail performs the dual roles of connecting *chaparral* and *desert* and highlighting the difference between them.

To get students to learn from text, then, we need to encourage them to process at a deeper level. We need to help them build connections among ideas and represent experiences at multiple levels. Unfortunately, many students fail to connect classroom tasks with real learning. In a long-term study in which researchers videotaped students engaged in classroom projects and activities and then asked students to report what they were thinking and doing, the pattern emerged that the students were "primarily engaged in managing the requirements of tasks"—that is, they weren't so much thinking about learning as they were thinking about getting an assignment done (Nuthall 1999a). If students perceive reading expository text as just a chore to complete, it is unlikely that higher-level processing will occur.

Structure and Features of Expository Writing

Text has a surface structure, signaled by the text features such as headings and titles, as well as an internal structure, or the relationship of main ideas to details. In *Summarizing, Paraphrasing, and Retelling*, I discussed several ways to help students become more aware of the surface structure of a text (Kissner 2006). Here, we will focus on how a text's internal structure shows the reader what to expect.

Students do seem to have an easier time with narrative text. Because narratives are told in chronological order, each sentence comes logically from the one before it, and students can make meaning at the local level. But in an expository text, each sentence relates back to the main idea, not necessarily to the sentence right before it. Students who are only reading at the local level, or using microprocessing, often fail to see how a whole paragraph fits together. Brendan is an example of this. In narrative text, he performed well. In expository text, his concentration on the details interfered with his ability to see how these details all related to a main idea.

What is text structure? Simply stated, it's the overall structure of a text, how the author uses the details to build a main idea. Expository text can be structured according to main idea/details, comparison, problem and solution, cause and effect, and description. Just like the different fiction genres, readers can develop a schema for each of these text structures. Each experience with a text will build the readers' understanding of how that kind of text works.

My students often come to me with very limited experience in understanding text structures. Using local-level processes of linking each sentence to the one before it, they think that they need to read every word of expository text. This makes the task of reading various sources about biomes and extracting information overwhelming. Eric looked at the pile of books I had gathered about the tropical rain forest, the biome his group had chosen to study. "Do I have to read all of those?" he asked in disbelief.

"Of course not," I replied. "Eric, you're studying animals, right? So as you read these books, you'll be looking for details about the animals of the rain forest."

He looked at me skeptically. Eric, like many students, had trouble seeing how the details of a passage relate to the text structure.

Often, the best clue to the structure of a text is the topic sentence. Many students just skip over the topic sentence, deciding that it is boring or unnecessary. But the opposite is true—usually, the topic sentence gives the reader a good sense of what details would follow. As I worked with students to read texts related to the different biomes they were studying, I knew I would need to teach them how to pay attention to how topic sentences signal a text structure. Knowing the details to expect in a paragraph would help them decide which paragraphs they needed to read.

To help students see this connection, I created sample topic sentences to use as models. When I shared these topic sentences with students, I explained how each one would lead me to expect different details. Here are the sentences I used for initial modeling, along with my explanations for each one.

"Although they have many differences, all three forest ecosystems share some common characteristics." This sentence seems to be telling me that three different kinds of forest ecosystems are similar, but different. I expect to find the names of the three forest types. I also think I'll find details about how they're similar to one another. It looks like this paragraph will be organized as comparison.

"Acid rain has become an increasing problem for the taiga ecosystem." In this topic sentence, the word *problem* shows me that I can expect to read about the problem of acid rain, including effects of the problem. This paragraph might have solutions, as well—I'll look carefully to see if they're included. This is probably a problem–solution paragraph.

"The cool temperatures of the taiga make decomposition a slow process." This topic sentence seems to be stating a cause and effect. In the rest of the paragraph, I would expect to see effects of the slow decomposition rate. This paragraph is probably cause and effect.

"The tropical rain forest is full of life." When I read this sentence, I think about things that are alive. I would expect to find examples of things that live in the tropical rain forest. I think this paragraph is going to use a main idea/details pattern of organization.

"Ooh, Mrs. Kissner!" said Eric, as I modeled reading aloud the topic sentences. "Can I see the rest of that paragraph? 'Cause I think it has information in it that I need."

Eric was showing a new awareness of how to use the topic sentences to figure out what the next details would be. After we read the sample topic sentences together, I directed students to look at our guided reading passage for the day—an excerpt from the science textbook. Working together, we skimmed over topic sentences in the book and talked about the kinds of details each paragraph might include. Students chose paragraphs that were most likely to include details about their individual topics, showing that they understood the relationship between topic sentences and details.

Flag Words

Topic sentences are not the only way that authors signal text structure or hint at details that are to come. Authors also use certain kinds of words to point to details. When I encountered the term *flag words*, I liked it, because I think it is more concrete for students than the more frequently used *transition* (Tomlinson 1995). The term brings to mind a flag in the text, marking something important. It's as if the author is saying, "Hey! Look at this!"

Just as students don't recognize the realistic fiction genre or read topic sentences, they also tend to skip over flag words. This leads to some big problems in their comprehension.

Think about the next sentence: "You might expect all forests to be the same. However, this is not the case." In this sentence, *however* is a flag word. It is a signal to the skilled reader that something different is coming—an idea that might not follow from what was previously stated. *However* is like a warning word, alerting the reader to an idea that might not make sense.

But my less skilled readers skip over the word. Instead, a student might read, "You might expect all forests to be the same," stop there, and conclude that all forests are identical.

I knew that students needed to learn how to use flag words to understand text. I created Flag Words Point to Details handout (Figure 9–1) to show students how different kinds of flag words will indicate different details. Using sticky-note flags, we went through the section in the science textbook, marking the different flag words and talking about their purposes.

When I found that the word *however* was still a problem for students, we took some time to practice writing sentences with the word. I put this on a dry erase board: "Mrs. Kissner was going to give the students weekend homework. However, . . ." and asked them to finish the second sentence. The students came up with some inventive sentences. Asking students to use flag words to communicate their own ideas helps to build their schemas for the roles that these words play.

Text Coherence and Comprehension

Expository text varies widely in its coherence, or how well ideas are linked together. As you choose text for student groups, pay close attention to the structure and coherence. A text that is poorly organized and lacks coherence poses a high degree of challenge for readers. In a study of sixth graders, incoherent text caused them to use mostly microprocessing

Flag Words Point to Details

If You Read These Words . . .	Look For . . .
first, **next,** **finally . . .**	A series of related ideas. These ideas may form a sequence or a chain of events, or they may just be a list. *Challenge:* Make sure that you understand whether this is a chain of events or a list.
most, **best,** **worst,** **funniest . . .**	Ideas or items that are being compared. These words are superlatives, or saying that one of the two things being compared is the most extreme in the group. *Challenge:* Make sure you know what is being compared.
therefore, **as a result,** **consequently,** **so . . .**	A cause and an effect. *Challenge:* Understand which event is the cause and which is the effect.
however, **despite,** **but . . .**	Something is different from what might be expected. *Challenge:* Understand why the next idea is unusual or unexpected.
like, **similar to,** **the same as . . .**	Two things are being compared. *Challenge:* Understand the similarities between the two objects or ideas.
on the other hand, **however,** **but . . .**	Two things are being contrasted. *Challenge:* Understand the differences between the two objects or ideas.
next to, **beside,** **on top of,** **near,** **to the left of . . .**	A description of how two things are related in space. *Challenge:* Make a picture in your mind.

FIGURE 9–1.

strategies, failing to make inferences and trying to simply recall information (Kintsch 1990). The next paragraph is an example of disorganized, incohesive text.

> There are several types of grasslands in North America. On the tall grass prairie, found in the eastern part of the United States, grass can grow to be five feet tall. The short grass prairie gets only ten inches of rain and grows next to the deserts. On the mixed grass prairie, grasses only grow to be two or three feet tall.

The different kinds of grasslands are described out of order, an organization that would interfere with students' making connections and inferences. To answer the question "Which kind of grassland gets the most rain?" less skilled readers would have a hard time making the inference.

Most text, though, has some organization. The next paragraph shows the same sentences but in a different order. However, it is lacking in coherence.

> There are several types of grasslands in North America. On the tall grass prairie, found in the eastern part of the United States, grass can grow to be five feet tall. The mixed grass prairie gets less rain and the grasses only grow to be two or three feet tall. The short grass prairie gets only ten inches of rain and grows next to the deserts.

Now the answer to the question is clear. The prairies are discussed in order from the tallest grass to the shortest, which implies that the tall grass prairie must get the most rain. But the best understanding seems to occur when readers encounter text that is both organized and coherent. In the next paragraph, the flag words are underlined. How do they show the connections between the ideas?

> There are several types of grasslands in North America. On the tall grass prairie, found in the eastern part of the United States, grass can grow to be five feet tall. The mixed grass prairie, <u>however</u>, receives less rain. <u>Here</u>, the grass grows shorter, only two or three feet tall. The shortest grass is found, <u>logically</u>, on the short grass prairie. This kind of grassland gets only ten inches of rain each year, and grows next to the deserts.

As I help less skilled readers understand the details of text, sometimes I rewrite articles to add more coherence. Adding flag words helps readers see the connections. When text is coherent, readers can make more inferences and better integrate information into their schemas.

Difficult Words

Difficult words can also have an impact on comprehension. In a study of sixth graders, researchers had two groups of students read two similar texts, one of which substituted difficult synonyms for words in the passage. Of course, students had more trouble understanding what they were reading in the text with more difficult words. But the students' understanding of the details seemed to suffer the most, especially understanding how each detail related to another. Students were able to get an overall idea of the meaning of the paragraph but had trouble seeing how the details related to the main idea (Stahl et al. 1989). Think about students who are using a textbook to study for a test. They may be able to show some generalized comprehension, but their understanding of the details may be impaired.

Understanding text structure, flag words, coherence, and the role of difficult vocabulary can help teachers match the right texts with the right students. However, the perfect text will be of no value if students don't bother to read it. For this reason, it's important to consider why students are reading the text—in other words, the context.

A Context for Reading: Providing a Task

There is one question that is like fingernails on the chalkboard for me. It comes after I have tracked down a text that matches my students' needs and reading abilities, designed lessons to go along with it, stood at the photocopier and made seven copies, and presented it in the most interesting way I could imagine. The question that I hate is, "Why do we have to read this?"

I must admit, there have been times when I have been tempted to say, "Because I said so." The demands of coming up with multiple texts can be exhausting. However, the students do have a valid point in wondering why they are reading a particular text. The purpose for reading, or the context of the reading experience, influences how a reader processes and understands a text. "Because I said so" is not the best motivator.

Quite a few studies have examined the relationship between the reader's goals and memory of details. An interesting one relates to participants reading a text about a house. In this study, undergraduate participants were assigned to one of three groups; all groups were given the same text about a house. One group took on the perspective of potential home buyers, who would be interested in the size of the house, the layout, and so forth. Another group took on the perspective of a burglar, who would probably look for information about the valuables in the house. The final group was not assigned a perspective. After they read, they had to recall information from the text. Each group assigned a perspective remembered more of the details that would be important to that perspective. Even more surprisingly, the perspective groups showed an increase in overall memory for details (Schraw, Wade, and Kardash 1993).

Not only does a reader's goal impact what is remembered, but it also affects what information is deemed important. In a text, importance is judged by many factors. Information can be of high *task-based* importance if the details are needed to perform a task—for example, details about the layout of the house was important to the readers who took on the perspective of home buyer in the previous example. But this is not the only measure of importance. A related measure is *personal* importance. Information that is personally important might relate to familiar places or experiences or address an issue in the reader's life. Finally, authors will mark important information by putting it at the beginning of paragraphs, repeating key ideas, and adding details to explain what's important. This kind of importance is called *text-based* or *textual* importance.

For the biome unit, my colleague Megan and I decided to give students a clear perspective for their reading. We decided that they would be learning about biomes in order to create hallway displays that would be used to teach sixth graders and kindergarteners. The perspective of reading in order to teach someone else is recognized as being highly effective in building readers' understandings of text. In order to explain information, readers need to create a richer knowledge base than if they were just reading for their own enjoyment (Coleman, Brown, and Rivkin 1997).

With perspectives in mind, we were ready to work with groups of students to explore the texts. We wanted students to take notes on important information, gathering enough details so they would be able to craft an effective paragraph about an aspect of their biome. We had taught about using topic sentences and flag words to help students find and understand details. We thought we were ready.

However, there was a subgroup of students in both of our classes who persisted in writing down every detail they could find. This is a common phenomenon with young learners. In *Summarizing, Paraphrasing, and Retelling,* I wrote about how to help students use text features to determine textual importance (Kissner 2006). Some of our biomes resources, though, had long chapters and dense text. Natalie, for instance, was researching how humans interact with the taiga biome. One book had a twenty-page chapter about the topic. I could have manipulated the text and made it easier. But there were six different groups of students working on different biomes—not only would it have been time-consuming for me to rewrite everything, but it would also have taken some of the challenge away from the activity.

Megan came up with an elegantly simple way to help students think about importance. She took her group back to the science text and said, "Today, we're going to read the section about the three types of forest again. However, we're going to pretend that we're only looking for information about the taiga. When we come to sentences or sections about the other types of forest, we can skip those." Together, they read the paragraph sentence by sentence. The students made a gesture of thumbs up when the sentence contained important details about the taiga and thumbs down when the sentence was not important. Then, students read aloud to a partner and did the same thing. One person read the sentences, and the other person decided if they were important, based on their perspective. With this activity, Megan took the task of determining importance out of the internal processes and into a shared context. This meant that students could draw on the background knowledge of one another, instead of being limited by their own experiences.

I decided to adapt this idea for a whole-group lesson on finding text-based importance. "Every sentence in a paragraph can be put in one of three groups," I told the class. "It's the topic sentence, an important detail, or a less important detail. Your job as a reader is to figure out which sentences contain the important details."

Together, we worked on the page called What's Important? (Figure 9–2). (In case you're wondering about the abundance of spittlebugs in my writing examples, I have to explain that my students from the past year were fascinated by them. I knew that tossing a spittlebug into a paragraph was a sure way to get their attention.) Many of my students thought that the first sentence was always the topic sentence. In this case, the first sentence is just a catchy little exclamation to get the attention of the reader.

"You mean the first sentence doesn't have to be the topic sentence?" Brendan asked.

"No," I said, and he nodded as if he had just learned something very important. I started to understand why he had done so poorly on the pretest.

"That's good to know," he grinned, and set to work on the rest of the paper.

In the paragraph shown in the What's Important? page, questions build some cohesiveness. Are these questions important? Not really. The questions function to help the reader link one idea with the next. Discussing the role of these questions, and how they relate to the other sentences in the paragraph, helped students see how they can evaluate each sentence to see if it is important to the text or the task.

I used a blank version of the activity (Figure 9–3) for guided reading groups. On this page, I simply handwrote some sentences from the texts that students were working with, and we revisited the whole-group lesson. Then, we went on to the more active style of thumbs up or thumbs down as they read more from different books about biomes.

As I mentioned earlier in the chapter, studies show that students often confuse task completion with learning (Nuthall 1999b). Trying to get an assignment done does not lead students to a deep processing of the text. When we give students a context for their reading by offering a perspective, they are more likely to remember important details and integrate new knowledge. The best test of true engagement is looking at what the students do on their own, without teacher prompting. As I sat down with

What's Important?

A paragraph can be taken apart so that each sentence can be examined carefully. Sentences can do different jobs in a paragraph.

- Topic sentence: States the topic of the paragraph
- Important details: Details that give new information that is important for your purpose
- Less important details: Sentences that don't carry information, repeat ideas, or are unnecessary for your purpose

Directions: First, read the paragraph.

"Ooh! Someone spit in that plant!" Maybe you've said this after seeing a glob of bubbly white foam on a plant. The culprit might be tinier than you think. A kind of insect called a *spittlebug* actually creates the foamy masses. Why would these insects do this? After the spittlebug nymphs hatch in May, they secrete a liquid. Then they move and twist their bodies around to whip this liquid into foam. The foam keeps them cool, moist, and hidden from predators. Pretty clever, huh?

Directions: Second, think about each sentence. Is it the topic sentence, an important detail, or an unimportant detail?

Sentence	Topic Sentence	Important Detail	Less Important Detail
"Ooh! Someone spit in that plant!"			
Maybe you've said this after seeing a glob of bubbly white foam on a plant.			
The culprit might be tinier than you think.			
A kind of insect called a *spittlebug* actually creates the foamy masses.			
Why would these insects do this?			
After the spittlebug nymphs hatch in May, they secrete a liquid.			
Then they move and twist their bodies around to whip this liquid into foam.			
The foam keeps them cool, moist, and hidden from predators.			
Pretty clever, huh?			

FIGURE 9–2.

© 2008 by Emily Kissner from *The Forest and the Trees*. Portsmouth, NH: Heinemann.

What's Important?

Directions: Copy sentences from the paragraph onto the table below. For each sentence, mark whether it is the topic sentence, an important detail, or an unimportant detail.

Sentence	Topic Sentence	Important Detail	Less Important Detail

FIGURE 9–3.

Bria, I noticed that she was working on notes related to two aspects of her biome: the climate and human interactions.

"Why did you decide to do two main topics?" I asked her, because the assignment had only called for one.

"There are only three people in our group, so no one was doing climate," Bria shrugged. "I thought it was something that people needed to know. I mean, how can you understand the tundra without knowing what its climate is like? So I decided to do it myself."

How would Bria's thought processes have been different if she were only reading the text to answer questions? This is a common task that we give to students. Although reading to answer questions does result in more recall than simply reading a text for no purpose, reading to perform a task seems to cause even more to be remembered (Geiger and Millis 2004). Clearly, the context of a classroom activity can change the very nature of our children's reading processes.

When students feel confident enough to take on new challenges, they have taken control of expository text. They can sift through pages and pages of text to find what is important. While Bria took the time to research an additional topic, she was also building her schemas for expository text, learning more about how text is structured and how to find details. As a teacher, I can provide text, help students figure out what is important, and give students a perspective for reading. In the end, though, there is only one person who can truly ensure that Bria processes text at a deep level: Bria herself.

The Reader's Prior Knowledge

As numerous studies and books have confirmed, prior knowledge plays a large role in understanding text. The brain is like a great mixing bowl of details. When the process works well, new details get folded into old details, building new schemas and creating new knowledge representations. When the process doesn't work well, new details may be remembered, but they just sit on top of the mixing bowl, unable to be used in meaningful ways. As you'll see, prior knowledge impacts the way students make inferences and remember information from text.

Making Inferences in Expository Text

My son Zachary has listened to more than his share of conversations about the reading process. Sometimes my husband and I underestimate the depth of what he picks up. One afternoon, as we were debating inferences in nonfiction, Zachary interrupted with a question of his own.

"Can you even make inferences in books that are real?" he asked. "I mean, it just tells you everything, so you're not trying to figure out a story."

My husband and I exchanged glances. This was some powerful thinking. "Do the authors tell you everything?" my husband asked.

Zachary replied, "Well, yes, they do. Like if the author says that a castle was built in a certain year, that's when it was built. You don't have to figure anything out."

I racked my brain to try to create an example of an inference in expository text. "Um . . . what about . . . the great architect Zachary planned the amazing Castle Dragon in 1207. He saw the results of his planning in 1217." My husband raised his eyebrows, but I shrugged. It was the best I could do on short notice.

"So? It took him ten years to build the castle," Zachary said. Then, "Oh! That was an inference, wasn't it?"

Inferences in expository text often feel quite different from the inferences we make in fiction text. Instead of making logical guesses about a character's traits, motives, and emotions, now readers are putting together ideas, bridging gaps in coherence, checking for plausibility, and considering causes and effects. Just like in fiction, however, expository text requires readers to make both text-based and reader-based inferences, and requires a substantial number of inferences per paragraph.

When information is just remembered word for word, it may not be available for making inferences. This information is called *inert knowledge* (Cote 1994). Yes, the details are there, but they're not usable. They're like deadweight in the brain. Consider the case of Andre, as he was taking a math test. He wrote a question mark next to the question "How many interior degrees are there in a quadrilateral?" As I talked with Andre later, I found out that he knew that a square was made up of four right angles. He knew that each right angle has ninety degrees. But this information was inert. Because it wasn't richly represented in his brain, he couldn't use it to solve the problem.

Many students have the mistaken idea that learning from text is the same as being able to remember information. However, remembering information from text entails a different process from making an inference (Durgunoglu and Jehng 1991). In order to be truly learned, information from the text needs to be integrated into existing schemas so that it can be pulled upon to make inferences and solve problems. Andre had only fragile links to the number of degrees in a right angle and the number of right angles in a square. He also had a shaky knowledge of what a quadrilateral was. Because this knowledge wasn't well integrated, it wasn't available to him to make a necessary inference.

Studies of how students learn in the long term suggest that making inferences is necessary for academic success. No matter how hard teachers try to make lessons link together and build bridges from one day's lesson to the next, there are times when information in a classroom is fragmented and isolated. Students manage to learn from this fragmented information by making inferences, synthesizing new information with old and building new knowledge structures. There seems to be a snowball effect to this—students who have greater prior knowledge will select more relevant classroom activities, which will give them more prior knowledge, which will be an advantage for future activities (Nuthall 1999b). Prior knowledge helps readers overcome problems in their comprehension as well. When readers enter a task with more highly developed prior knowledge, they are better able to make inferences (Durgunoglu and Jehng 1991).

I can't give all my students the rich background experiences they may be lacking. I can, however, teach them how to make the most of what they have. By showing them how to use their prior knowledge in reading expository text, I hope that I can help them make rich connections across the curriculum.

Recognizing Prior Knowledge

Students often fail to recognize the inferences they are making. In addition, they often don't add new information from a book to their schemas. I used the picture book *In the Woods: Who's Been Here?* to help students understand how they can use and add to their prior knowledge (George 1995).

Although this is technically a fiction book, it sets the reader up to make real-life inferences about animals in the forest. The picture book is quite simple and has two children going through the woods and seeing signs of animals. Every few pages, the book shows some clues and asks the question, "Who's been here?" On the next page, the reader sees the creature that left the clues.

To activate the students' prior knowledge, I first asked them to make a list of animals they knew lived in the temperate deciduous forest. This was important to link to our study of biomes, because I wanted the students to be able to link what they knew about the forests around our homes with understanding biomes. (When I did this, I hadn't yet discovered the related book by Lindsay Barrett George, *Around the World: Who's Been Here?* [1999]. This would be another book to link new information with old.)

After students made their lists, we started to read the book. On one page, the children come across a nest in a tree. "Who's been here?" the text asks.

"It's a bird," guessed Lindsay.

"Yeah, but a special kind of bird who makes a nest like that," Bria said, pointing out the way the nest hung down from the branches. When we turned the page, the picture of the northern oriole was revealed.

"Can I add that to my list?" Samantha asked.

This was exactly what I had wanted to happen. Students recognized that they could use information from their prior knowledge to make inferences from text. But they also saw that they could add new information to existing knowledge.

"I didn't have any birds on my list," Matt said. "I'm going to add some more, and see if they're in the book too."

On another page, I drew students' attention to how they were making inferences to try to figure out which animals had left the signs. "Something left bits of pinecones and seeds on a rock. What animal do you know that can do that?"

Students suggested chipmunks, mice, and squirrels. The next page showed that the creature had been a red squirrel. "You used your prior knowledge of animals in the forest to make an inference about who had left the seeds," I told students.

Contrary to what people will tell you, the process by which new information is learned and stored in long-term memory is quite complex and somewhat mysterious. What information would the students remember from this lesson? How would this information be available to make future inferences? We really don't know. This is what makes teaching an art instead of a science. Making the process of adding to prior knowledge transparent and visible to students does seem to add to their ability to infer (Hansen 1981). If students know how the process works, it seems, they may be more likely to use it.

After we read the book, I asked students, "If I asked you to make a list of animals of the temperate deciduous forest now, would your list be longer or shorter than before?" This question led to a conversation of how the book had added to students' prior knowledge.

"I never even heard of a goshawk before," Maggie said.

"That part about the family of foxes was cool," Thomas added. "I didn't know foxes ate groundhogs."

Does one lesson cause a lightbulb to go on in the reader's head? Does she see the error of her ways and promise to use prior knowledge from now on? It would make teaching easier. However, students need to be exposed to information over and over again, in multiple ways, in order for it to be well remembered. Teaching students how to use prior knowledge to make inferences and how to add to prior knowledge is unlikely to have much effect if they're only done once. For students to learn how to synthesize information, they need opportunities to experience the process over and over again.

After we finished the biomes unit, we worked on a social studies unit to study modern Chinese culture, learning about etiquette, food customs, and other aspects of everyday life. On the third reading selection in the unit, I asked a guided reading group to write down words they expected to find in an article about the history of chopsticks.

On the top of his paper, Thomas wrote *fan*. I was shocked. *Fan*, the Chinese word for grain, had been explained in passing in the first article we had read. I hadn't drawn the students' attention to it, and we hadn't really discussed it as we worked on the text. But Thomas had known it was important. "I decided that this word might be in the article because the other article we read said that the Chinese ate *fan* at every meal," he said. "If we're reading about chopsticks, it'll probably tell about food also."

As it turned out, *fan* was included in the article. The other students were impressed at how Thomas remembered a detail from two weeks before. So was I! Over the rest of the year, I saw the snowball effect of teaching children to pay attention to their prior knowledge and how they make inferences. A reader knows more about a topic, so the reader can remember details more effectively and make interesting inferences. This makes the topic even more interesting and causes the reader to seek out more information. Students who start learning keep learning.

Conclusion

It's clear to see how the reader, text, and context overlap. The reader needs to understand the words in the text and represent them richly, processing at the level of the situation model. If the text is disorganized or not coherent, the reader might not be able to make sense of the information. If the text has too many difficult words, the reader might not see how the details relate to one another. If the task is not motivating, or if the reader is applying a measure of personal importance instead of task-based importance, then the reader might not put together ideas. And if the reader does not integrate new information with prior knowledge, details may be stored but not available for future use. A simple reading task can be very complicated!

Fortunately, there are many things teachers can do to help students process text at a deep level, make sense of the details, and make the details available for future inferences. Here are the big ideas that I keep in mind as I plan for instruction.

Things to Remember About Teaching Text Structure

- Texts have a surface structure and an internal structure.

- Inexperienced readers often try to read only at the local level, trying to connect each sentence with the one immediately before it instead of looking for the macrostructure of the text.

- The topic sentence of a paragraph often shows the structure and, in turn, what details to expect.

- Flag words highlight important details to the reader.

- Struggling readers have trouble with text that is disorganized or lacking coherence.

- Advanced readers seem to work harder to understand text that lacks coherence and may use more sophisticated processing.

Things to Remember About a Context for Reading

- A perspective for reading helps readers remember details.

- The goal of reading to perform a task causes more recall than reading to answer questions.

- Information in a text can have textual importance, as signaled by the author, task-based importance, importance for a future task, and personal importance.

- Students can learn how to distinguish between important and less important details.

Things to Remember About Prior Knowledge

- Learning from a text involves synthesizing new information with old, reorganizing existing schemas.

- Inferences in expository text often depend on prior knowledge.

- Information that is remembered but not available for inferences or problem solving is called *inert knowledge*.

- Students need to make inferences every day, just to put lessons together and make sense of school.

- Helping kids see how they use prior knowledge to make inferences can improve their skills.

10

When the text, the context, and the reader come together, readers can learn from text. They can add to their prior knowledge and become more enlightened individuals, lifelong learners, passionate students . . . well, you get the idea. Things are good. But there are times when other problems get in the way. These barriers to learning all have one thing in common: they are based in details.

Wait! Aren't details good? Yes, of course, the right details are important to learning. When readers activate the details in their brains and integrate those details with new information from text, everything works out well. But sometimes there are contrary details that just don't want to behave. Sometimes students have prior knowledge that just isn't compatible with the text. Their prior knowledge contradicts the details in the text, leaving students confused and unable to integrate new information with old. Finally, seductive details can pull a reader away from main ideas and important details in a text.

Incompatible Prior Knowledge

It's a well-known fact that children develop unusual explanations for the world around them. Often, they don't talk about these ideas; they just assume that everyone else thinks in the same way. We can sometimes get a glimpse of their thinking by asking direct questions. "Aidan, Zachary is eight right now. How old will he be when you turn three?" I asked my toddler. He looked at me seriously and said, "Gacky be two!"

Aidan definitely has a different idea of how ages work. Students also bring interesting and unusual ideas to the classroom. Many of my students are firm in the belief that a sentence should never start with *because*. This was one of the first things they learned as emerging writers, and they cling to the belief. I might say that sentences can start with the word, and I might show them examples of how authors structure sentences, but what they learned in second grade is too ingrained. Their prior knowledge interferes with how they learn new experiences.

For students, much of their wrong information might come from their own mistaken inferences, like Aidan's assertion that Zachary was going to be two years old next year. Many students also think they have learned these things from their parents. The charitable side of me hopes that parents aren't intentionally filling their children's minds with wrong information and that the kids misinterpreted what they have heard. Over the years, I've been told that copperheads and black snakes have cross-bred, leading to a poisonous black snake (not true), Denver's weather is warmer than ours because it is closer to the sun (not true), and wind can carry the rash-causing oils in poison ivy (never proven).

When readers read texts that are incompatible with their existing views of the world, they experience a contradiction. Students who activated faulty knowledge before reading a text that contained incompatible knowledge performed more poorly on targeted test items than those who did not activate prior knowledge, suggesting that faulty prior knowledge may lead to worse comprehension than no prior knowledge at all (Alverman, Smith, and Readance 1985). I have seen this effect in my own classroom. Before we read an article about microbes, one group of students became very stuck on the idea that microbes cause disease. The text, on the other hand, explored the uses of microbes in decaying waste and making foods like cheese and yogurt. After they read the article, some students became convinced that they would get sick from cheese and yogurt. Their prior knowledge caused them to make a faulty connection between details.

I attribute learners' difficulties with giving up mistaken information to two different reasons. It wouldn't be at all useful for readers to flit back and forth from opinion to opinion, constantly trading in old facts for new ones as they read different texts and encounter new ideas. So there is an adaptive reason for keeping prior knowledge. To children, the information that is oldest and most securely tied to schemas is clearly the knowledge to keep. When we read the article about microbes, students made an incorrect inference in an attempt to keep their prior knowledge and allow for the new knowledge.

The second reason for keeping prior knowledge is simpler. I think that no one likes to be wrong. To incorporate new information into our schemas, we need to admit to ourselves that something is lacking in our current thinking. Students who shy away from academic risks find this very discomforting.

But when students disregard new information in favor of their prior knowledge, they lose opportunities to learn from text. They have trouble integrating new ideas. When unresolved inconsistencies are stored in long-term memory, the links are fragile, meaning that the knowledge is not richly represented and is easily forgotten (Nuthall 1999b). Obviously, this does not make for good learning.

We might conclude that it's best to avoid activating prior knowledge when it seems likely that students will have misconceptions. But how can we know about the faulty prior knowledge that students bring to texts? In my undergraduate science methods class, the professor suggested that we interview every student before every unit to find out what students already believe. This idea seems almost laughable now. Of course there is no time to do this in the real world of the classroom.

In the end, I think that it's not as important to know students' misconceptions as it is to teach students how to deal with them. Mistaken ideas and faulty prior knowledge are just facts of life. As knowledge changes and evolves, sometimes we discover that what we previously thought is not the case. Students need to learn how to deal with conflicting information.

This ability to integrate new information and transform schemas, in fact, has been shown to be a factor in determining interest in adults. That is, skilled adult learners often seek out and enjoy learning information that runs counter to their prior knowledge and requires them to transform their schemas (Yarlas 1999). I've seen this same effect in students who become immersed in a topic. Rather than ignoring inconsistencies between texts, they find the tiny little details fascinating. How can we cultivate this kind of interest?

Dealing with Inconsistencies

Opportunities for Predicting and Confirming
The real-life classroom activities discussed back in Chapter 2 can help students develop the habit of seeking new information, reorganizing their ideas, and transforming their existing schemas. Whenever students are led to make and check predictions, they gain vital experience in dealing with inconsistent information.

For example, before we walk on the nature trail, we often predict what we will see. These predictions are based on our prior knowledge of the season, the trail, and the weather. As we're outdoors, we have an immediate chance to check our predictions against reality.

I model this process by sharing my own thinking. One day in late February, Carly predicted that we would see robins. "I haven't seen any yet this year," I told her. "I think it's still a little early. I've never seen any before March."

But when we went outdoors, Carly called to me. "Mrs. Kissner! Look! I told you there were robins now!" Sure enough, there was a robin, hopping across the grass.

"I guess they are back," I admitted. "You've convinced me. The robins are back, even though it's only February. I'll have to remember that for next year." Then I added a question that I had. "I wonder what causes them to come back at different times? It would be interesting to track that over several years."

This tiny conversation is just one example of how our own attitudes about new information can set an example for students. When we show that we are willing to make changes in our thinking, we demonstrate the habit of mind of allowing for new information. By following up with a question, I showed how new information can cause us to think in new ways. The more chances that students have to see how new information can be learned, the more interesting they will find the process.

Explicit Teaching

Informal conversations are great ways to help students understand how to deal with conflicting information. As I work with students on research, however, I find that students need some more formal instruction about how to deal with information that conflicts with their own prior knowledge, as well as conflicting details from multiple texts.

I knew that I needed to address this issue when Natalie came to me as she was studying native plants. "Mrs. Kissner, one of these websites is wrong," she said. "On one, it says that serviceberries grow to be twenty feet tall. On the other, it says that serviceberries grow to be fifteen feet tall. Which one is right?"

Together, Natalie and I looked at the websites. One was from a state department of forestry, while the other was from a student's research. "Which one do you think is more reliable?" I asked Natalie.

"Well, I guess the forestry place. Forestry is where you study trees, right? So they would know."

Natalie had come up with a way to resolve the inconsistencies she had found in the texts. I decided to design a lesson on the topic for the whole class to study. I used her experiences as the framework for a lesson with the entire class. The Collision Course page (Figure 10–1) explains what readers need to do when they come across information that contradicts what they already know.

When authors are aware that a fact goes against common knowledge, they often leave a clue for the reader. Words like *however* and *despite*, flag words discussed in the previous chapter, are examples of this. There are also longer phrases that point to facts or details that might surprise a reader. With the next lesson, we made a list of these phrases, and then sought out new ones. Here are some of the examples that students found:

- You might be surprised that . . .
- People often don't know that . . .
- Contrary to popular belief . . .
- Although many people think that . . .

Incompatible prior knowledge can keep some students from learning new details and understanding new information. By meeting the problem head-on, we can help our students avoid this problem and learn how fascinating it can be to explore details beyond our schemas.

Seductive Details

Dealing with incompatible prior knowledge can be challenging enough. Dealing with seductive details can be even harder.

Collision Course
When Your Prior Knowledge and the Text Don't Agree

Sometimes you will read text that includes ideas that might not go along with what you think you already know. What does a good reader do?

Recognize when you see a fact in text that doesn't agree with your prior knowledge.

Think about why this might be so.
- Where did you originally learn this information? Is it a reliable source?
- What are you reading now? Is it a reliable source?

Decide what to do.
- Trust your prior knowledge, and ignore the new information in the text.
- Decide that the information in the text is more reliable than your prior knowledge.
- Look for more information in other reliable sources.

Directions: Here are some situations that students might encounter. In each one, think about whether the reader should trust prior knowledge, go with the new information, or seek another opinion.

1. Beth's cousin told her that toads give people warts. In a field guide to reptiles and amphibians, Beth read that this is not true.

Keep prior knowledge? _____

Why or why not? _____

_____

2. At a nature center, Max read an exhibit sign that said that wetlands are important for the environment. In an old encyclopedia, Max read that wetlands are just homes for mosquitoes and should be filled in.

Keep prior knowledge? _____

Why or why not? _____

_____

Directions: Can you think of a time when you had to choose between your prior knowledge and new information? What happened? What did you decide?

FIGURE 10–1.

A classroom study of the rain forest helped me see the problems of seductive details. To help them generate some topics about the rain forest, I had given a group of students about twenty minutes to look through a variety of lushly illustrated books and magazines.

"What are some things that you noticed?" I asked, my marker poised to record ideas on the chart paper.

Brett raised his hand. "There's a tree in the rain forest that has diesel in it."

Well, this was a surprise. "Really?" I asked.

Several other students agreed. "It's in a magazine," Casey said. She brought me a copy of *Kids Discover.* "Here," she said, and pointed. Sure enough, it said that the copaiba tree had diesel fuel in it.

"Interesting," I said, resolving to research that detail myself. I was having trouble adjusting my schema to allow for diesel fuel running through the leaves of a tree. "I'll write that down. What else did you find?"

"I've heard that you can make gas from restaurant grease," Andrew offered.

"Is the oil in the leaves, or in the bark?" Jessica wondered.

I sighed. The detail of the diesel fuel in the tree had proven to be so seductive that it lured students away from a deeper understanding of the rain forest. (As I discovered in my later research, the South American copaiba tree does contain a substance that can be refined into diesel fuel.)

Seductive details are those details that pull a reader away from the main ideas of the text. These details usually have some key points in common. They are often unexpected, with surprising information, and have a strong appeal to the senses. Seductive details usually relate to interesting topics like danger, death, chaos, romance, and sex (Shank 1979). Although they can be fun to read and remember, they often impair a reader's understanding of the main ideas and important details of the text. For example, a study of skilled adult and seventh-grade readers found that both groups had more trouble remembering the main ideas of paragraphs that included seductive details. Even more problematic was the fact that seventh graders who read the seductive details had trouble remembering other details as well (Garner, Gillingham, and White 1989).

Why do seductive details have such disruptive effects? They may interfere with how readers determine main ideas. Many seductive details are only tangentially related to the main idea of a paragraph and are not easily subsumed, or integrated, into the main idea. The reader is then not sure of what the author was really trying to say (Garner, Gillingham, and White 1989). Additionally, seductive details may cue readers into activating the wrong prior knowledge. When my students started talking about oil from restaurant grease, they had strayed far from the rain forest. They were using prior knowledge, but it wasn't the prior knowledge that would help them with the task.

As with incompatible prior knowledge, the best way to deal with seductive details is to confront them. Students need to know that these details are out there, and that as readers, they can control whether they pay attention to these details or not.

I use the Details, Details page (Figure 10–2) to show students how different paragraphs can have different levels of detail. Even though all the paragraphs have the same ideas, the third one includes several seductive details. With the class, I discuss how those details do not add to the main idea. We discuss how the words pulled the students away from the text instead of helping them understand the main idea.

Seductive details are not just problems in students' reading. A study showed that seductive details in lectures interfered with the students' abilities to remember information and solve problems (Harp and Maslich 2005). There is, of course, a distinction between an interesting idea that supports the lesson and a seductive detail that pulls readers away from the lesson.

This has led me to reconsider my own instruction. It's hard to know the boundary between a detail that supports an objective and a detail that will pull us away. The decision-making process is even harder when students raise their hands to talk. Will they make a comment that is on track? Will it distract us all?

In guided reading one day, I gave an off-topic conversation two minutes to unfold, just out of curiosity. We were discussing Robert Frost's "Nothing Gold Can Stay." To lead students toward the theme, I asked them if they had ever had a gold time in their lives. Can you see where the seductive details hijacked the conversation?

Brad said, "When I had a cat, and she was like, my best friend, and she slept in my room every night, that was a gold time. Then she died." He was quiet for a moment, thinking. "I think maybe the theme might be enjoy it while it lasts, because it might not be there. Like if you have a pet, it will probably die before you."

Shannon put in, "Not really. What if you get a pet when you're ninety?"

Ian added, "Parrots can live to be, like, fifty years old."

Brad just stared at them. Conversations can quickly be overtaken by seductive details. Without my intervention, it's impossible to guess where this discussion would have gone. The topic of pets' longevity was infinitely more interesting to some students than the theme of the poem. If I allow these conversations to go too far, students may get in the habit of always reaching for topics that are tangential to the text. This will get them into some interesting conversations in the short term. In the long term, though, this habit will pull students further and further from well-developed comprehension.

The idea of how seductive details can impair understanding in both text and lectures has also led me to think out my prereading ideas very

Details, Details: What's Important?

Read the three passages below. Which one:

- has unimportant details?
- has seductive details?
- has the best details?

Be ready to discuss your choices.

A

If you want to find out if a stream is healthy, try looking for stream-dwelling creatures. Some creatures can only live in high-quality water. If you find mayfly nymphs, water pennies, or caddis fly larvae, you can be sure that your stream is clean and healthy. Other creatures can survive in water with some pollution. Crayfish and dragonfly nymphs can live in streams that are not perfectly clean. And there are some animals that can live in even very polluted water! If the only creatures you can find are leeches and aquatic worms, the stream is probably in trouble. By finding out what creatures live in your stream, you can decide if the water is polluted or clean.

B

If you want to find out if a watery stream is healthy, try looking for stream-dwelling creatures. You can do a stream study with simple equipment like nets, ice cube trays, and magnifying glasses. Some creatures can only live in high-quality water. You can find these creatures by getting into the stream and looking under rocks. Other creatures can survive in water with some pollution. If you are looking under rocks, make sure that you replace whatever you pick up. And there are some animals that can live in even very polluted water! By using nets and other tools to find out what creatures live in your stream, you can decide if the water is polluted or clean.

C

If you want to find out if a stream is healthy, try looking for stream-dwelling creatures. Some stream creatures can only live in high-quality water. The mayfly nymph, a creature with three tails, can be found wriggling under rocks. Others can survive in water with some pollution. You might find a crayfish as long as your finger, waving his claws. To catch a crayfish, just remember—they swim backward. There are some animals that can live in even very polluted water! (Watch out for leeches!) By finding out what creatures live in your stream, you can decide if the water is polluted or clean.

Figure 10–2.

carefully. Activities that go along with a text but do not reinforce the main ideas have not been shown to aid comprehension (Stahl et al. 1989). These kinds of activities proliferate in reproducible books and on the Internet. Before reading about life along the seashore, for instance, students might be prompted to make a list of what they would take along on a beach trip. Although this has a slight connection to the text, it would not reinforce the main ideas. Students might remember details about the prereading activity at the expense of the details from the article. A better prereading activity in this case would be something that directly correlates to ideas from the text—for instance, matching names and pictures of creatures mentioned in the article.

Interesting details that relate clearly to the goals of the lesson, however, are desirable. How can we tell the difference between seductive details and useful details? I encountered a great example in late May. My husband and I, who happened to be teaching across the hall from one another, decided to swap classes. I would take his class for a hike along our school nature trail; he would teach my class the standard long division algorithm.

When I returned from the nature trail, I asked my class what they had learned. I naively expected to hear an in-depth analysis of how standard long division differs from the partial quotients method students had previously learned. So I was somewhat surprised when Matt said, "Every puppy's precious!"

"Okay," I said, confused. "Weren't you learning about long division?"

"Every puppy's precious," Andrea explained. "When you're dividing you could go out to a decimal, but if you're dividing something like puppies, that would mean that you have to cut up the puppy, and that would be bad."

"And messy," Abigail put in.

Andrea continued, "So you have to think about what you're dividing, and decide if you want to go to a decimal or get a remainder."

Oh! Now it made sense. I wished that I had been able to see the lesson myself. In this case, the interesting detail of the split-apart puppy served to reinforce the content. It was a vivid image that sparked a memory to an important concept of problem solving in division. Instead of seducing learners away from the main ideas, it helped to highlight them.

"Can he teach us again tomorrow?" Thomas asked. "He made math fun." Realizing the implications of his words, he added, "Not that you're not fun, but—well, it's almost the end of the year, and we're tired of the same old thing, and—you know what? I think I'll just stop talking now."

Conclusion

As I worked with students to improve their comprehension by becoming aware of inconsistencies between their prior knowledge and the text, learning about their emotional reactions to text, and understanding the power of seductive details, they responded in typical sixth-grade fashion. When Shannon and Scott noticed that some marbles went down the marble ramp at a faster speed than others, Scott remarked, "That's really odd. I thought they would all go at the same speed. I'm going to have to try to figure out why that's happening." And when Brendan was reading a page out of his science textbook, he covered up one of the detailed diagrams. "I keep on wanting to look at the picture, but it's not related to the main idea," he said. When students know about the pitfalls of reading expository text, they can overcome those problems and gain a better understanding of what is really going on.

Things to Remember About Prior Knowledge

- Prior knowledge that is incompatible with a text can lead students to impaired comprehension.

- When students don't connect inconsistent information, they are more likely to forget details.

- To help students resolve these conflicts, model thinking about where the prior knowledge was obtained, how reliable the source is, and whether the new information is likely to be more reliable.

Things to Remember About Seductive Details

- Seductive details pull a reader away from the main ideas of a text.

- By emphasizing themes like danger, death, chaos, and romance, seductive details interfere with how young readers process both main ideas and details.

Quick note: What interesting fact do you remember most clearly from this chapter? If it's the fact that the copaiba tree's oil can be refined into diesel fuel, you've had firsthand experience with the memorable power of seductive details.

WHAT WE KNOW ABOUT KIDS, DETAILS, AND TESTS 11

The week of state testing always makes me feel like a stranger in my own classroom. Cherished displays are taken down or covered, desks are rearranged into stark rows, and our comfortable, usual routine is disrupted. Several students leave the classroom to take the test with individual or small-group accommodations, leaving our group incomplete. I can only plan scattered, fragmented activities to fit into the times between testing, and the usual friendly atmosphere of the classroom is shattered by our need to follow test protocol and security.

Nervous excitement fills the air. Students have come to see the tests as not totally unpleasant, because they do get free breakfast, snacks, and an afternoon of movies or games. In my state, students do not get results back until the end of the next September, so they don't really see a correlation between their work on the test and any real consequences. Some students are really motivated to do well, while others just see days of drudgery stretching out before them.

I'm nervous too. By my own assessments and my own measures, I can see that students are making progress. I can see that what I am doing is working. But without a stamp of approval from a disconnected, external authority, all my work will seem like it is for nothing. On top of this feeling of insecurity, I am also deluged with new details of my own, like which students go where for accommodations, when I am to hand out snack, and where I put the carefully sharpened pencils.

A test scenario is quite different from the way that reading usually happens in my classroom. Instead of humming with quiet (and not so quiet) talk, a testing room is silent. Students cannot talk to each other about ideas, background knowledge, or questions. They cannot share knowledge or build rich connections between multiple sources.

A test situation, then, is inherently different from ordinary instruction. Sadly, some teachers think that matching instruction to the test will improve students' performance. Lessons become filled with silent test preparation activities that students complete from workbooks or sitting in front of a computer screen. These lessons do teach something, and scores do seem to improve. But are students really improving at the underlying processes of reading, or are they just improving at answering questions? Does it matter?

Obviously, I think it does. I would hate to give up taking kids outdoors so that I could squeeze in more workbook time, or keep kids from choosing independent reading books so that I could do more teacher-directed lessons, with every student reading the same text at the same time. Not only would this deprive students of meaningful experiences, but it would also teach them to view school—and learning—as tiresome drudgery.

I want to have my cake and eat it too. I want to teach reading in the social, interactive, and individualized way that I have come to love, but I also want students to do well in the rather artificial environment of standardized testing. In order to achieve these almost contradictory goals, I need to know as much as I can about the nature of testing. How does the context of the testing environment affect how students understand details? What can we do for students who are reading below grade level? Answering these questions can help us build a classroom environment that nurtures creativity and independence while preparing students for the rigors of standardized testing.

Effects of a Reader's Goals on Processing Details
In regular classroom instruction, students read text for a variety of reasons. Sometimes they choose a book simply because it looks interesting. Sometimes they read to gather information about a topic or participate in a conversation. And sometimes they read a story because I assign it.

On standardized tests, though, students read text for one purpose and one purpose only: to answer questions. The thinking behind this is simple. If students are good readers, they will be able to show their strong comprehension by selecting correct answers and constructing responses. But this view fails to account for the fact that the purpose for reading actually affects how readers approach a text.

We know that a reader's goals can impact comprehension. Reading to perform a task, for instance, results in a more sophisticated level of understanding than simply reading to answer questions. This might be due to the fact that reading to perform a task engages a reader in picturing the steps. Such imagery would involve the use of the situation model, causing a deeper level of processing than simply reading to form a textbase (Geiger and Millis 2004).

In addition, when readers are given a perspective for reading, they remember more important information from the text (Schraw, Wade, and Kardash 1993). When college students were assigned to read a text with the goal of being able to explain it to someone else, they seemed to create a richer understanding of the text than those who read for other purposes. The students who were going to explain the information connected new information more strongly to old and came up with more illustrations of how the concepts worked (Coleman, Brown, and Rivkin 1997).

Obviously, a reader's goals influence comprehension by dictating how readers process, store, and connect important details. How can this impact student performance on tests? Because students are reading just to answer questions, they may use more shallow processing than when they read for more authentic purposes. Without prompting from the teacher or peers, students might be content to just process words at the surface and textbase level, constructing a literal understanding of the text but failing to create a situation model. This may lead to impaired comprehension, as students are not drawing on background knowledge to build rich inferences and mental images. This is bad news for test scores.

Classroom Activities to Help Readers Set Goals for a Text

Although people who create and administer tests may think that all students will work to their fullest potential on every test, those of us who spend time in the classroom know that this is not the case. And I think that test scores may lead people to incorrect inferences about students' abilities, assuming that just because a student *didn't* show deep processing on a test item means that the student *can't*. In the world of real readers, though, there is clearly a distinction between the two conditions of *chooses not to* and *is incapable of*. Sometimes readers who are very capable just don't process text to their full potential.

The reader's goal for reading influences how deeply students think about the text. In my everyday instruction, I work with students to process text at a deep level. I engage my readers in reading to perform a task, adopting varying perspectives on a text, and explaining ideas to other readers. On a test, though, I am unable to use any of these strategies. I'd love to tell students, "Read the stories on the test today. After we hand in our test booklets, we'll discuss the stories in small groups. Your job will be to retell the story from the viewpoint of another character." Unfortunately, although these directions could result in enhanced comprehension, they could also get me fired. Test security demands that we do not discuss the stories, poems, or articles on the test—ever.

I can hope that students will have become so accustomed to processing at the level of the situation model that it becomes automatic. Indeed, for some readers, it does. But these are long tests, with students reading three and four selections in one session. There are so many details to notice, connect, and remember that even the most engaged readers can feel their motivation start to flag. In these cases, then, I need to provide students with coping strategies that fit the demands of text security and that will also lead students to process the text more deeply.

The task becomes even more challenging because I can't actually tell the students to do any of these things under test-taking conditions. Once I've handed out the test booklets, I have to become Crazy Test Lady, the person who reads from a script and doesn't help students. So these coping strategies need to be fairly simple and easy to remember. I cue students to do these strategies by walking around with a clipboard. "During the test, I can't tell you to do things that will help you to understand what you read," I tell the students. "However, when I walk around with my clipboard, I hope that you will remember to do these things."

Pause and Picture Images from the Text

When readers picture images from the text, they go beyond literal processing and into the rich world of the situation model. Visualizing is an easy-to-understand strategy that can lead to improved understanding. Whether students are reading narrative or expository text, mental images can have a strong effect. When students make pictures in their minds, they are synthesizing new details from the text with what they already know.

Pretend to Retell the Story to Someone Else

This strategy adapts the immense benefits of retelling to a testing situation. Obviously, students can't actually talk to another student about a text they read on a test. But they can shift the verbal activity to a mental one and pretend to retell the story. It helps for some students to have a little stuffed animal on their desks as a pretend audience. When students retell a story, they have to think about how all the details fit together, restructuring and reorganizing their thinking.

Highlight Main Ideas and Important Details

I introduce this with some caution. All too often, prompting students to highlight leads to beautifully decorated papers, sneakers, and fingernails. However, my state's rules allow the use of highlighters, as long as they are used in classroom instruction. While I worked with readers to identify important and unimportant details, then, I allowed them to use highlighters of different colors to mark the relative importance of details. Choosing what to highlight gives students a reason for examining details closely and paying attention to what is most important.

Granted, these strategies are simple. They are not meant to be instruction, but cues to help students remember the skills they have already learned. By walking around with the clipboard, I remind students to use these strategies. As I go around the room, I do write down the names of students that I see working well. I recognize their efforts at the end of the day with a low-budget version of Let's Make a Deal, in which they can choose from coupons for various classroom prizes. Although I do not usually give students prizes for classroom performance, a test situation offers little in the way of authentic motivation for students, making it necessary for me to offer some extrinsic motivations.

Effects of Time on Processing Details

Whether students must complete a test under a time constraint can have a real impact on their performance. Time constraints can interfere with how students understand details, including how they match pronouns to antecedents, understand words, and integrate ideas.

Of course, not all reading tests have time constraints. In my home state of Pennsylvania, for instance, students are allowed to go beyond the suggested window of time and theoretically work on a test until the end of the school day. In other states and on other tests, however, students must read selections and answer questions within a time limit—some rather short and some rather long.

Does the amount of time that students have to complete a test really make much of a difference? For some students, it doesn't. Students who are fluent readers, who have well-developed vocabularies and adequate working memories, will perform well under both conditions. But there is a group of readers for whom the time limit can be devastating. Students who are not automatic in one or more reading subprocesses—for instance, students who are not fluent readers, or those who have difficulty matching anaphors—will show less comprehension on timed tests.

A reason for this has been suggested by Jeffrey Walczyk. According to the Compensatory Encoding Model, or CEM, readers can compensate for ineffective reading processes by using compensatory behaviors or strategies. Some compensatory behaviors include looking back in the text, rereading, pausing, subvocalizing, or slowing down the reading rate. With these compensations, even readers who are having problems with some of the smaller processes of reading, such as decoding words, can come to a literal understanding of the text (Walczyk 2000).

One example of an effective compensation is pausing during reading. Studies have shown that readers often pause at the ends of sentences, probably to integrate the ideas with the preceding text. Some readers also pause before reading multisyllabic words, probably to spend some more time decoding. Another compensation is rereading. Readers often reread when they encounter problems with anaphoric relations (remember those pesky multiple referents) or when they are distracted by the reading environment.

These compensations take time, which is why those of us who face untimed standardized reading tests are at a distinct advantage. When readers are constrained by time, those who have poor subcomponents of reading skill, like poor working memory or decoding skills, do poorly. However, when readers are freed from time constraints, those with less efficient subcomponents are just as likely to gain a literal understanding of the text as those who can process text more efficiently (Walczyk et al. 2004).

Research supports this idea. For example, when third and fifth graders had to complete a reading task with a time restriction, their comprehension was limited. Predictably, the more fluent readers—those with more developed reading subskills—performed better. However, when students read without the time restriction, comprehension improved. The less fluent readers had the time they needed to carry out their compensatory behaviors and presumably looked back in the text, paused, and reread (Walczyk and Griffith-Ross 2007).

How does this impact testing? Obviously, timed reading tests will put some of our readers at a severe disadvantage. Because they are not able to use compensatory behaviors, they will not be able to correct confusions in the text. They may not understand key details, may fail to use details to make appropriate inferences, and may miss out on important ideas. Under time restrictions, these students will appear to have poor comprehension.

However, although these students will seem to have poor comprehension on a timed test, untimed classroom measures can tell a different story. Jack, for instance, had serious fluency and decoding issues and could barely stumble through a timed reading passage. However, he loved to read on his own. When I saw him reading *The Lord of the Rings* trilogy, I worried that he was trying to read something too difficult (Tolkien 1965). But some conversations with him revealed a different story. Not only was he able to explain how the book was different from the movie, but he was also able to explain why the books were appealing to him. "They're filled with such neat details. Like the battle scenes—I can really picture myself there." When we discussed other books and stories as a class, Jack was able to make creative, thoughtful insights and show a deep level of comprehension. In this case, a timed test could not show the real picture of Jack's reading capability.

Classroom Activities to Help Students
Understand Details on Timed Tests

First, the good news: There is evidence that slight time restrictions may increase motivation for many students, as they create a more challenging context. Even if you are not preparing your students for a timed test, then, it might make sense to do some activities under moderate time restrictions. Helping students read with more speed and accuracy is always a good thing.

But simply reading faster is not enough to ensure that students will understand the details they encounter. I noticed this as I was doing some quick fluency probes in my classroom. They sounded so simple—time the child reading for one minute and count the number of words that were read. However, I soon realized that if students only read what they could get through in one minute, they would experience only pieces of text. This is not the lesson that I wanted to teach. I needed to change the structure of the fluency activities so that students could make sense of the details.

Preview a Timed Reading

I want students to understand that it is worth the time it takes to preview a text. Whether a reader is working with a time restriction or not, it is important to take a short period of time to look over a text. This is just standard practice for reading teachers, who teach many different lessons about previewing and predicting. But a mixed message is conveyed when the teacher sits beside a student and pulls out a stopwatch. Few students have the courage to speak up and say, "Could I just look over the text before I begin? It will improve my comprehension."

Therefore, we need to explicitly tell students that it is okay to preview a text before a timed reading. This can be done as a timed or an untimed activity. For example, I have said to a student, "Good readers preview a text before they read. I'd like you to take one minute to look over this text and see if you can figure out what it is all about." Most students finished previewing before the time was up. I have also told students, "Take a moment to preview this article before I hear you read. See if you can figure out the structure of this text." Then, I waited until students indicated they were ready before starting the timed reading.

How does previewing help students understand details? Put quite simply, a preview of the text gives details a place to live. By looking over the text, students can activate their schemas for both the kind of text and the topic of the text. This will help students attach meaning to the details they encounter in their reading.

Connect Details to Main Ideas with Timed Text

This is a fairly simple technique that can be tossed into regular classroom instruction. After students read a timed text, ask them to explain the relationship between a detail and a main idea. At the individual level, this can be a simple question. In the beginning of the year, students often look at me blankly when I ask them to do this. "Why do you think the piece of rusty metal that Lonna finds is so important?" I asked Melissa, after she had read aloud for one minute and then completed the text on her own.

Melissa looked at me, looked at the paper, and raised one eyebrow. "Because it was in the story?" she guessed. Melissa had read quickly and accurately, but I could tell that she was not making sense of what she read. I couldn't let this continue.

"That's not enough of an answer," I told her. "When you read, it has to make sense. Look back to the story and try to figure out why the piece of metal was important. Here, let's look together." This one-on-one teaching moment did take longer than if I had just listened to Melissa read for a minute and written down her score. But it resulted in much better comprehension. After several weeks of quick fluency probes and simple questions, students showed improvement. Compare Melissa's performance to Matt's.

"How were the donkeys important in the story?" I asked Matt, when he was done.

He frowned slightly and seemed to think for a moment. "Well, the customs guy thought that the man was using the donkeys to smuggle something, but it turned out that the donkeys are what the guy was smuggling." Even with a time constraint, Matt was able to read and understand the details of the text.

Reading under time constraints can impair the comprehension of any learner. This brings us to the next question. On standardized tests, how can learners identify and correct problems with comprehension?

Effects of Reading Problems During Testing

The testing environment is not a normal one, for many reasons. In the course of regular instruction, students and I talk frequently. Often they ask me for help with figuring out words, understanding concepts, or deciding on a course of action. I am not the all-knowing giver of answers, but I do try to steer students in the right direction, pose some questions to get them thinking, or make suggestions of how they might solve a problem.

While we are testing, however, I can't do any of these things. I am not allowed to give students any guidance toward choosing or creating an answer. This can create some uncomfortable moments for students during testing, as they must solve all of their problems on their own. Constructing meaning is no longer a shared, social activity. Of course, I don't believe that eliminating social learning activities from my classroom is an appropriate strategy for test preparation. However, I do need to equip students with some specific coping skills to help them deal with the unique set of challenges posed by tests.

Classroom Activities to Help Students Identify and Solve Reading Problems

Solving comprehension problems requires two distinct processes. First, students need to recognize that a problem exists. Then, they need to select an appropriate strategy to solve the problem.

Practice with Inconsistencies

When children are reading, a problem with reading a single word can often snowball into a more global problem with the text. For students in Chapter 7, substituting *canyon* for *cannon* caused their visualizations to go offtrack. If readers do not correct these problems, they can fail to understand the entire piece of text.

Helping students notice problems, then, is very important. Researchers have devised an interesting way to see how readers self-monitor as they read, using texts with inconsistencies to detect self-monitoring behaviors. For instance, a text might mention that the weather is stormy in one section, and refer to the bright sun in another section. If a reader pauses or rereads at the point of the inconsistency, it can be inferred that the reader noticed the problem and is trying to resolve it.

As I tried to devise lessons for helping students notice problems with text, I considered creating some inconsistent texts like the ones used in research studies. However, I decided that this course of action was a little contrived. I don't want kids to think that comprehension problems stem from errors in the text. Usually, these issues arise because of a reader's misunderstanding. I decided to go with a simpler tactic, one that I could use easily during read-aloud.

"As I read to you today," I instructed my class, "I will be making one mistake on purpose. I want you to listen carefully and see if you can find my mistake." Students leaned forward attentively, eager to be the ones to find my error. I quickly added, "Don't raise your hand or call out right away. Instead, keep listening until I stop."

Because I wanted my error to be similar to one that students might make in a natural reading situation, I skipped a line of text. This is an error that I often hear students make, and one that can really make a passage difficult to understand. After a moment, we discussed the error. How did they determine my mistake? How did it affect an understanding of the passage?

To keep students listening for inconsistencies, I continued to toss in some small errors every now and again. Besides helping students figure out problems in text, it also provided an excellent cover for those times when I really did misread something.

Once students find problems, they need to resolve them. A reader with a comprehension problem faces several choices. It may be a problem with the text, a problem with how they read the text, or a problem with the interpretation of the text. When students are faced with many texts and a limited amount of time in which to read and understand them, they are understandably reluctant to embark on long, difficult procedures for working through comprehension problems. Therefore, I like to model some very simple strategies for dealing with inconsistencies.

Model Rereading

Distractions happen, in the regular classroom environment and on tests. For example, our latest round of tests was punctuated by three deer running along the edge of the field outside our window. When readers are distracted, an appropriate compensation is to reread the last sentence or two. I make it a point to model this during read-aloud. When I am interrupted by an announcement or an expected visit, I go back and read the last sentence before going on. This shows students that they can easily slide back into a text after a distraction.

Purposes for Pausing

I can always pick out the students who have had a heavy dose of timed fluency training. When I ask them to read aloud, they start with a gulp of air and then barrel aggressively through the text, racing against the clock to get in as many words as they can and they just can't stop or even pause for the end of a sentence because they have to go fast.

I think that this is counterproductive. Reading with fluency is important, but instruction must go hand in hand with an emphasis on meaning. In addition to asking kids questions to help them see the relationships between main ideas and details, I also emphasize elements of prosody and accuracy over speed. "You know, it's good to pause," I told Andrea, conversationally.

"It is? I thought I was supposed to keep reading," she said.

"Pauses help you understand what's going on," I explained. "When you get to the end of a sentence, you need to take a second and put it all together. Pause, and then go on."

She raised her eyebrows at this, but complied. When the sentence was done, I asked, "Now, what was that about?"

"Well, there was this guy who was smuggling something, and then . . ." she rattled off. Looking surprised, she said, "I guess I did understand it better that way."

Conclusion

The weeks of standardized testing transform our classrooms from pleasant, comfortable learning spaces into tense, silent test sites. Students' performance on the test does not just depend on how good my teaching has been that year, but on complex interactions of my readers' goals, feelings, ability to suppress incorrect answers, reading skills, and writing skills.

I know that students learn best when the classroom is a place where details are valued, talked about, shared, and examined. I refuse to simply become a test preparation coordinator. I think that the best confirmation of my approach could be found in the attitudes of the students. As I walked around to help students, Jose called me over and pointed to a description of an experiment that was in his test book. "Mrs. Kissner, can we do this?" he asked.

I frowned at his test booklet, noting that this passage hadn't appeared in every book. Did that mean that it was new or old? I didn't know and couldn't take the risk. "I don't think so," I said.

"But it would be fun! I want to find out what will happen," he persisted.

I remained firm in my denial. At lunchtime, though, I had to intervene in another conversation between two students who were discussing what they had read on the morning's test. "You can't do that!" I told them. They looked at me in surprise. "You're not supposed to talk about what you read," I added.

"Oh," they said, disappointed.

For these students, reading had become something more than just decoding the words and finding the right answer. They actually enjoyed the process of reading and processing new text, thinking and talking about the details and what they liked. I was having my cake—and eating it too.

What to Remember About Kids, Details, and Tests

- The testing environment affects how students process details.

- Prompting students to use deeper processing strategies on tests can lead to improved performance.

  - Picture images from the text.

  - Pretend to retell the story.

  - Highlight main ideas and important details.

- Time constraints can have a negative impact on performance, as students will not be able to use compensatory strategies.

- There are several strategies to help students get to better comprehension with timed tests.

  - Take the time to preview the text.

  - Connect details to main ideas.

- When students have trouble reading a passage, they may misunderstand important details.

  - Helping students notice inconsistencies in a text is one way to build self-monitoring skills.

  - Teaching students to pause and reflect on what they have read can also help them to find and fix problems.

12 DETAILS ON MULTIPLE-CHOICE TESTS

"Today, you're going to take a short reading assessment," I announced to my class. Their faces fell. As I handed out the tests, though, several students brightened.

"Oh," Mark said, sighing in relief. "It's just a multiple choice!"

"No writing?" Crystal asked. "Whew!"

Most kids respond favorably to multiple-choice tests, thinking that they're getting off easy. And kids aren't the only ones who find the format easier. Multiple-choice tests are quite popular, for obvious reasons. They're easy to administer, easy to take, and easy to score. It seems like a win-win situation for everyone.

In reality, though, readers need to go through a pretty complex process to correctly answer multiple-choice questions. First, they need to read the text itself, activating relevant prior knowledge and constructing meaning at the textbase level and creating a situation model. Then, readers need to read and understand the question. The next step is to read each one of the possible choices and check to see if it matches with an understanding of the text. If the question requires an inference, the reader might have to generate that inference using details from the text. The reader may not find a match in the listed choices, which would require the reader to then go back into the text to search for a correct answer. The reader will also have to suppress a recognition response to answers that might contain correct information but do not necessarily answer the question.

And this is getting off easy?

Talking About Multiple-Choice Tests with Students

To get an inside look at what it is like for your students to take these kinds of tests, try giving them the article "Starting Out with Sled Dogs" (Figure 12–1) and the accompanying questions (Figure 12–2).

Searching for a Detail

Some multiple-choice questions require a reader to go back to the text to find an answer. But some students were unwilling to do this.

"You know, you are allowed to look back at the story to answer the questions," I told Samantha as she took a practice test.

Starting Out with Sled Dogs

If you like dogs and the outdoors, you may want to become a "musher."

Thinking about racing with sled dogs? It can be a fun-filled, exciting sport. People in many states are exploring the world of racing with dog teams.

But before you head into the Arctic tundra, it's important to learn as much as you can about caring for your dogs and communicating with your team.

The Right Dog

Just about any kind of dog can be trained to pull a sled. Some breeds, though, are more suited to the sport. Everyone imagines the husky as the classic sled dog. The Alaskan husky, although not recognized by the American Kennel Club, is one of the most popular kinds of dogs for racing. The Siberian husky grows to be a little larger and is almost as popular. It was recognized as a specific breed by the American Kennel Club in 1930. Finally, Samoyeds are also suited for pulling sleds. The Alaskan malamute, while not suited for racing, is a powerful dog, good at pulling heavy loads.

If you are buying a dog, it's important to find one that is smart and obedient. An older dog who has been a good leader but is getting too slow for an adult musher's team might be perfect for someone who is just starting out.

Caring for Your Dog

Did you know that some mushers have their own special recipes of food to feed to their dogs? Even if you don't go to the trouble of chopping up special combinations of meat, you can still keep your dog healthy with nutritious dry food. Read the instructions on the bags of food and weigh your dog to make sure that you are feeding him the right amount.

Table scraps and other human food treats are not good for dogs. However, mushers do enjoy giving their dogs treats after a race.

Water is important for dogs. Sled dogs get very thirsty! Mushers sometimes give their dogs "baited" water before a race. This means that they put some yummy meat juice in with the water so the dogs will drink it all.

Most sled dogs don't need a great deal of fancy grooming. Simply keep them clean by brushing their fur, wiping off their paws, and giving them occasional baths.

Training Your Team

Don't expect to say "Mush" to make your dogs go! Modern racers don't use that term anymore. Instead, they will say "Hike" or "All right" to tell their dogs to run or go faster.

Simple commands like "sit" and "stay" are good places to start. You can teach the dog that "gee" means turn to the right and "haw" means turn to the left. Do this by letting the grass grow tall in parts of the yard. Mow some paths with turns and intersections, and then practice taking your dog through it with a leash. If your dog masters the leash training, try hooking him up to a harness and letting him go in front.

After awhile, you will be ready to graduate to a real sled. Dog sleds are quite different from the sleds you use to get down a hill. Check out used sleds to see how they work and which features you prefer.

If you enjoy the outdoors and love working with dogs, mushing might be a sport for you!

FIGURE 12–1.

Multiple-Choice Questions

Directions: Read each question carefully. Circle the best answer.

1. This passage is organized so that it mostly
   a. explains the causes and effects of racing sled dogs
   b. compares sled dogs to house pets
   c. gives information about choosing and caring for sled dogs
   d. describes the problem of mistreating sled dogs and offers possible solutions.

2. As used in this passage, the word <u>suited</u> means
   a. inappropriate
   b. dressed up
   c. happy
   d. appropriate

3. Which of these is a fact?
   a. Most sled dogs don't need a great deal of fancy grooming.
   b. Table scraps and other human food treats are delicious for dogs.
   c. The Siberian Husky was recognized as a breed by the American Kennel Club in 1930.
   d. Everyone imagines the husky as the classic sled dog.

4. Which is a heading in the article?
   a. Caring for Your Dog
   b. Starting Out with Sled Dogs
   c. If you like dogs and the outdoors, you may want to become a "musher"
   d. The Siberian husky is a popular breed of sled dog

5. Why is it important to choose a dog that is smart and obedient?
   a. These dogs are easier to care for and don't require fancy grooming.
   b. Smart and obedient dogs will be easier to train to pull sleds.
   c. Older dogs may not be fast enough to pull sleds for adults.
   d. Dogs that are not obedient may bite you.

FIGURE 12–2.

"I know," she said. She worked on steadily, reading the questions and filling in answers. She did not flip back to the story.

"Then why aren't you looking back at the story?" I asked, after she had filled in another wrong answer.

She wrinkled up her nose and shrugged.

I took away the option. "For this next question," I told her, "you must go back to the text and show me where you find the answer."

Samantha seemed to comply, reading the question to herself and turning the page to go back to the story. Then she looked up and asked me a question very typical of sixth graders. "Can I go to the bathroom?"

What is it about searching for answers that brings out such avoidance behaviors? When students don't have an effective search strategy, they often will just guess at an answer—or, as in Samantha's case, try to avoid the task all together. There are a variety of search behaviors that yield varying levels of success. One of the least effective strategies is going back to the beginning of the text and rereading the entire thing. When a student does this, it's a clear cry for help. This student didn't build a textbase in reading, and probably has only a limited comprehension of the text.

An only slightly better strategy is an undirected search. A student doing an undirected search will zip around in the text, guided by whatever thoughts are zooming by. A student who is searching randomly has probably seen the search strategies of more effective readers. However, without a clear representation of the order of ideas, this undirected search is unlikely to be successful.

One effective strategy for searching is skimming. A reader who skims goes quickly through the text, just glancing at words and phrases until the desired section of the text is found.

But the best searchers are those who are able to go right to the correct point in the text. It's no surprise that these readers, the ones who can find details quickly and effectively, also show great comprehension. In order to understand what leads these readers to the right detail, it's interesting to see what happens when strong readers are asked to perform under adverse conditions. When good comprehenders are presented with a scrambled text, their advantage evaporates, and they can no longer find details as quickly as with a well-organized text. This tells us that readers' memory for where to find information is related to the structure of a text. Strong readers know that the structure of a text can help them find the information they seek (Cataldo and Oakhill 2000).

Does it help to have readers try to imagine how a page looked? Although people often speak of being able to "see" where a key fact was located on a page from a textbook, evidence suggests that this is not true. Readers find information by using cues from the sequence of a text, not place-on-page memory. Suppose you had to look back in this text to find information about kinds of inferences. You might remember that it comes fairly early in the book, after the introduction and before the information about visualizing. The memory for the sequence of ideas in a text is quite strong and seems to be formed at the level of the textbase or the situation model (Therriault and Raney 2002).

To sum up, then, students may choose from a variety of strategies to find a detail in text. The least successful strategies are random searching or rereading, and skimming or using the text structure are strategies that lead to better results.

Classroom Activities to Help Students Search for Details

I don't want my students to feel like they are looking for elusive needles in the haystack of text. Teaching the skills needed for effective searching on multiple-choice tests can fit seamlessly into everyday instruction. The first step to helping students improve their search strategies is to do some simple observations. Are students performing an undirected search, simply looking over the entire text? Do they go back to the beginning and reread the whole thing? Or do they try to avoid the task, like Samantha?

Teach Skimming and Scanning

Skimming and scanning are two distinct processes. Skimming requires the reader to go lightly through the text, jumping from one idea to another and skipping over trivial details. Scanning, on the other hand, is looking for a specific word or phrase in the text. Both are equally important and have different applications.

The first question from the sled dog article refers to the overall structure of the text. Therefore, skimming seems appropriate. I show students how they can skim by reading the headings and the topic sentences only. In a well-written and considerate text, this should give the students the information they need to answer a question that requires them to find the text structure or main idea of an article.

Scanning is a great technique to teach to help students find key words from a selection. As we go over new vocabulary words, for example, I will write the word on a dry erase board and then have students scan for it in the text. They are able to come up with some interesting ideas about scanning. Proper nouns, for instance, are easier to find, because the capital letters stand out in the text. Long words also seem to jump out at students. The second question from the sled dogs article prompts students to do an easy scan. The underlining of the word causes it to stand out in the text.

Require Students to Find the Answer in Text

Although kids hate to look back in text to find the answer to a question, requiring students to search for information in the text has been shown to improve the performance of poor comprehenders (Cataldo and Oakhill 2000). In guided reading and whole-group lessons, I toss in some questions that require students to skim or scan and then tell them to highlight or underline the place where they find the answer, or the information that helps them infer the answer. When students practice this, they realize that going back to the text to find an answer is not as difficult as they previously supposed.

Finding details is a major challenge of multiple-choice tests. But not all questions require a reader to use a simple detail from a text. On many questions, students must use the details from the text to generate an inference.

Using Details to Make Inferences

Not all answers are directly stated in the text. Often, students will need to use details to build inferences. Although some inferences are formed while readers are engaged in the reading process, other inferences, especially predictive and elaborative inferences, will not be made until the student encounters the question. For some students, this is an uncomfortable feeling, as they look at a question and realize that they can't choose an answer.

"But I don't know the answer," Jenny said, as we did test preparation activities. She shoved the paper away. "I'm just stupid."

Students like Jenny need to know that inference questions require a different kind of thinking. "You don't have to know the answer right away," I told her. "Think about what the question is asking. Use the information in the text to help you come up with an answer, and then see if it matches any of the choices."

Question 5 for "Starting Out with Sled Dogs" is an example of a question that requires an inference. A student who tries to search for the phrase *smart and obedient* in the text will not find the answer to the question. Because this is a reader-based inference, the reader must connect the detail about smart and obedient dogs with other details from the text to conclude that smart and obedient dogs will be easier to train.

Classroom Activities for Helping Students Use
Details to Answer Inference Questions

When teaching students about making inferences to answer questions, no test preparation strategy can substitute for good, solid instruction. Students who want to read to learn more about the world will find the task of making inferences much easier than those students who view reading as a chore. In addition to test preparation strategies, then, I want to make sure that I teach students how to notice the details in texts and how to use these details to build both reader-based and text-based inferences.

Teach Students About Question–Answer Relationships

Teaching kids about question–answer relationships (QAR) is one way to help them see that not all answers can be found in the text. With QAR, answers to questions can be categorized as "right there," "think and search," "author and me," or "on my own" (Raphael and Pearson 1985).

Questions that require inferences, then, usually fall into category of "think and search" or "author and me."

QAR has been adopted by a number of standardized test preparation programs and can be combined effectively with regular classroom instruction.

Scaffold Students to Find Answers

This approach is useful for students who have problems with searching as well as forming inferences. I help them narrow down the options by focusing their attention on the specific paragraphs that contain the key to the inference. As students improve and begin to feel more confident, I open up the search, moving first to pointing to multiple paragraphs, then to showing a page, and finally to telling whether the information is found at the beginning, middle, or end of the text.

When Details Don't Help: Suppressing Incorrect Answers

Finding details and generating inferences do not always guarantee success. Poor readers face still another problem with multiple-choice tests. Sometimes, their understanding of the text and knowledge of the details can stand in the way of choosing a correct answer.

To understand how this works, look at question 5 of Figure 12–2. The correct answer to this question requires an inference about why smart and obedient sled dogs are preferable. The other three answers contain true information but are not answers to the question. As distractors, they are quite attractive. After a study of how skilled and less skilled readers make suppression judgments at tests, Debra Long, Mark Seely, and Brian Oppy concluded, "To the extent that selecting the appropriate answer requires suppressing the inappropriate ones, less skilled readers may be particularly disadvantaged. This disadvantage, however, would result from activities that occurred at test, rather than those that occurred (or failed to occur) during comprehension" (Long, Seely, and Oppy 1999). This means that our less skilled readers may have good comprehension of a text but still choose the wrong answer to a question because of their difficulty with suppressing attractive distractors.

Classroom Activity for Suppressing Incorrect Answers

As we went over a group of practice questions, Matt sighed in frustration as he marked his fourth wrong answer. "I knew that," he muttered.

Much of the writing about tests and testing discounts the fact that there are real children taking the tests, with real feelings. Matt's fragile confidence in his growing reading skills was undermined each time he realized that he chose an incorrect answer. Think about the frustration!

Students who are having trouble suppressing incorrect answers are the students who seem to understand what they read but fall apart on multiple-choice tests. These children need to know that they can read and comprehend but that the format of the test can interfere with their answers. Once I understood the problems they were facing, I had to come up with some ways to help them.

Formulate Answers Before Reading Choices

As I worked with a guided reading group to read through some state assessments, I was dismayed to see that some students were marking answers before I had even read the directions. "Don't mark your answers yet," I told Connor.

He looked up guiltily and put the pencil down. When I continued with the directions, he furtively picked up his pencil again, looked at me, and marked yet another answer.

Clearly, my instruction was not going to have much of an effect as long as the students were so intent on just marking answers. For the next session, then, I was prepared. I gave students the reading selection and the questions. I put each possible answer on a different sheet of paper that I could easily display.

"Sometimes, when we take multiple-choice tests, we find that there are several possible answers that might be true. There might be answers that use the details from the text in a way that sounds correct. However, there is only one best answer to the question. The problem is, when we are trying to take the test quickly, we might be tricked into choosing an answer that is not the best answer for the question," I told students. Connor gave a shamefaced smile. "To help avoid this, the best solution is to slow down. Let your brain do some thinking first to try to make up an answer. Then, look at the answers that have been provided for you, and see which one is the closest match to what your brain says."

Lisa was nodding. "Just like what we do in math," she said. "We're not supposed to look at the answers until after we've solved the problem."

"Exactly!" I said, pleased that she had made such a good connection. "Let's try it with a few questions." After they read each question, I gave them a moment to try to create an answer. Then, I displayed the choices. This led to a rich discussion of how the wording in answers might be confusing and what to do if the answer in your mind doesn't match any of the choices.

For the next few sessions, I slowly gave control back to the students. Next I gave them the questions with the answers covered by a self-stick note, along with the directions to leave the note there until they had come up with an answer. In the next session, students covered up the answers with their hands until they had formulated a response.

Conclusion

"You know, Mrs. Kissner," Thomas told me, "everyone thinks multiple choice is easy, but it's really not. There are lots of tricks you need to remember."

Multiple-choice tests present many challenges for students. Not only do they have to be able to search for correct answers, but they also must connect those details to form inferences, while also managing to suppress incorrect answers. It's no wonder that many test creators have turned to another format for testing reading comprehension: the much-loved, much-hated constructed response, which is the focus of the next chapter.

Teaching About Details on Multiple-Choice Tests

- Students may use different search strategies to find answers to questions: rereading, undirected searching, skimming, and going right to the correct answer.

- Teaching students how to skim and scan the text can help them improve their search method.

- The strongest readers use a memory of the text structure to find specific details.

- Requiring students to locate the place in the text where the correct answer can be found is associated with improved performance.

- Some questions require students to build inferences.

- Certain readers may know the correct answer to a question but have difficulty suppressing attractive distractors.

DETAILS IN CONSTRUCTED RESPONSES 13

In the previous chapter, I shared how students are often quite relieved when they look at a reading assessment and see the comforting letters of multiple choices. I see the opposite reaction when I pass out an assessment that requires students to write a response.

"Look at all those lines!" Caleb marveled. "Do I have to fill them all up?"

"Not all of them," I said.

"How many, then?" he asked. Before I could answer, he started spouting out numbers. "Ten lines? Twelve lines?"

I looked at him. "You have to fill up as many lines as it takes to answer the question," I said.

He returned my gaze, chewed on his eraser for a moment, and looked back down to the paper. "Ten lines would be good," he said.

I took a deep breath. I had only four months before my entire worth as a teacher would be decided based upon how students like Caleb answered these constructed-response questions. And he wanted to know how many lines he had to write? Obviously, Caleb didn't understand how important it was for him to use details in his response. I needed to change his view of these questions—and fast!

The Need for Details in Constructed Response

Constructed-response questions require a reader to build a response. The reading tests for at least thirty-four out of the fifty states include constructed-response questions, as well as current versions of the Terra Nova and NAEP. Although each test uses a unique format for the questions and their expected answers, students everywhere have to support their answers to reading questions with details from the text. Most questions require students to form an inference, make a broad statement, and then support that statement with specific examples from the story or essay. Some tests also require students to explain how the story details they choose relate back to their general statements.

A constructed-response question requires students to coordinate many different reading skills, most of which require the use of details. First, students need to use the details in the text to form an inference. So students are going from looking at details to looking at big ideas. But the

153

thinking doesn't stop there. As they write their responses, students must go back to a detailed view, tracing back through their thinking to identify the details they used to build the inference.

Suppose a student read a short story about a character named Mandy. If a question asks the students to name a character trait of Mandy's, it is not enough to simply say, "Mandy is kind." Instead, the character trait *kind* must be supported by specific examples from the text. For instance, students could explain how Mandy shares her lunch with others, how she helps the teacher pick up papers in the hallway, or how she reads a book to her younger brother. These are the "critical facts" from the passage that led to the inference. Depending on the test, students might also be expected to explain the rule that governs the inference. In this case, students would need to explain what the trait *kind* means and show that the examples support this trait. This requires students to consider the details once again, in yet a different way.

Why Constructed-Response Questions?

These questions obviously require some heavy-duty thinking. They are included on tests for several reasons. Constructed-response questions do eliminate the suppression problem that less skilled readers might face on multiple-choice tests. That is, less skilled readers sometimes have trouble eliminating distractors that are true but do not answer the question. When students write their responses, they do not have this problem.

Besides eliminating the suppression problem that less skilled readers might experience with multiple-choice tests, constructed-response questions are also supposed to measure a deeper aspect of reading than multiple-choice questions. By combining reading and writing, constructed-response questions are thought to provide a measure of a reader's literacy skills as opposed to just their ability to select a right answer (Jenkins, Johnson, and Hileman 2004).

Most rubrics for constructed-response questions disregard writing conventions and writing style, focusing instead on whether the reader included an answer to the question and enough text detail to support that answer. However, writing skill has been shown to influence the quality of a reader's responses. In a study of how students performed on multiple-choice questions, constructed-response questions, and writing assessments, the students' writing skill was shown to contribute to their ability to frame constructed responses (Jenkins, Johnson, and Hileman 2004). This means that our students who have trouble with writing will be at a disadvantage when it comes to these kinds of questions. On some tests, students have a very limited space in which to write answers, as well as limited time for reading and planning. This only increases the challenge and the likelihood that writing skills will count for just as much as reading.

Uh-oh.

Student Problems with Constructed Response

My own experience with constructed-response questions has been frustrating. I have worked in both Maryland and Pennsylvania, two states that require students to write constructed responses with specific text details. Getting kids to include these specific details, though, can be devilishly difficult. It's not that teachers haven't tried. I've seen acronyms, graphic organizers, combinations of graphic organizers *and* acronyms, videos shown every morning, skits, everything short of dancing monkeys, trying to get kids to write these text-based details to support their answers to reading questions.

And heaven knows that I have tried. I've used the graphic organizers, put up posters with the acronyms, and even considered wearing a dancing monkey suit to teach the children about the graphic organizers and the acronyms. I've modeled, I've scaffolded, I've shown examples on the overhead projector for us to score together. I've used blue highlighters to highlight text-based details, pink highlighters to highlight general statements, and yellow highlighters to highlight transitions. But even with all of this instruction, some students still did not include the necessary details.

One of the most troubling problems I noticed was an underdevelopment of responses. Students would answer the question with just one or two sentences but fail to support their response with the specific details from the text. Obviously, these students had noticed and used the details in the text to build their general statements. But they were not able to trace back through their thinking to explain how they used these details to build their generalizations. The issue wasn't with their reading ability, but with their ability to move quickly from big idea thinking to detailed thinking and back again.

I'm not the first person who noticed that students have trouble with constructed-response questions. Back in 1992, researcher Sandra McCormick launched an impressive study of how students with reading disabilities approach inferential short-answer response questions. From the responses of eighty students to a variety of questions from narrative and expository text, she was able to explore the most frequent source of error (McCormick 1992).

In the study, some students relied too much on background knowledge, ignoring text information in favor of what they already knew. Given how readers often fail to integrate background knowledge with new text details, this is not surprising. A possible explanation for this is that because less skilled comprehenders may not be processing the text at a deep level, they simply don't have as many of the details from the text available to them in their working memory, causing them to rely on prior knowledge instead.

Another common problem turned out to be an underdevelopment of responses. Students in the study often failed to develop their answers.

On high-stakes tests, a child who *didn't* provide the necessary development of an answer is assumed to be *unable* to do so. But is this really the case? I began to suspect otherwise as I observed my students carefully. When I added more lines for their answers, or even put bullets to show that I expected a certain number of text details, their responses improved markedly.

Not all responses in the study were underdeveloped. Some were too specific, pulling on details from the text instead of the ideas needed to support the inferences. Background knowledge is probably a factor in this kind of response as well, especially because this kind of response was seen twice as often in expository text as narrative text. Without enough prior knowledge, students may have simply copied information from the text.

Finally, some students made responses that were unrelated to the question. Instead of making and explaining an inference, students just wrote summaries of the text or wrote down some random details (McCormick 1992).

If you have read a number of student answers to constructed-response questions, all of these problems probably sound familiar. Armed with the knowledge that I wasn't alone in these problems, and an awareness of the kinds of problems that students often face, I could make some changes to my instruction to help students construct the best responses. Most of my students could already make the inferences required. I needed to teach them how to make their constructed responses showcase their reading skills, by including the right specific details.

Understanding Specific Details

Many children can parrot the word *specific* but cannot explain what makes a detail specific or not. It's a tough concept. Before students can write responses that include specific details, though, I need to be sure that they know what specific details are.

I capture examples of specific thinking whenever I see them. Helping kids to improve with their constructed-response questions, then, is not just something that occurs in the two weeks before the test. We work on this kind of thinking when we notice details on the nature trail. We improve with specific details when we explain why we gave ourselves certain ratings on self-monitoring, when we write character sketches, when we explain how certain details led us to make inferences.

To help students integrate their implicit understanding of "specific details" with the requirements of constructed-response tasks, I created Specific or Not Specific? (Figure 13–1), a simple activity that has students decide whether certain sentences are specific details or not. I've adapted this activity to a multitude of texts. With narratives, I include sentences that don't include the names of characters or specific settings. For expository text, I intersperse specific details with more general statements.

Specific or Not Specific?

Directions: Read the ideas from the article "Starting Out with Sled Dogs." Beside each one, circle *specific* if the idea is a specific detail or *not specific* if it is not specific.

Racing is fun.	Specific	Not specific
Samoyeds, Alaskan huskies, and Siberian huskies are good racing dogs.	Specific	Not specific
Dogs need food.	Specific	Not specific
Some breeders add meat juice to water so dogs will drink it.	Specific	Not specific
The dogs can learn how to do lots of different things.	Specific	Not specific
In the summer, you can practice racing with mowed paths.	Specific	Not specific
Some dogs are good for racing.	Specific	Not specific
It's important to know a lot of stuff when you want to race sled dogs.	Specific	Not specific

Directions: We can use specific details to support ideas. Find details to support this idea: The dogs can learn how to do lots of different things.

Detail 1:

Detail 2:

FIGURE 13–1.

A key component of this activity is to include some statements that could go either way. The exact categorization of these sentences is not the important part of this activity. What is important is how the students discuss the relationship of these ideas to the text, deciding whether each one is specific or not. With each dispute, students can share their background knowledge and build their schema for the writing genre of constructed response.

Leading Students to Write Constructed Responses

We start working with constructed responses early in the year. I introduce the basic format with Writing a Constructed Response (Figure 13–2).

Our discussion of problems with constructed responses is usually quite lively. Students actually know when constructed responses are not well developed. What they don't know is how to improve them.

Reading the Question

I included a short list of steps for students to follow. These steps come from my experience with helping kids write responses. First of all, I need them to read the question carefully. Students who are used to answering only one kind of question—for instance, summarizing a text—may need a great deal of work with understanding how the structure of the question will lead to an answer. Underlining the important parts of the question requires students to make an active response. Often, students drift into an autopilot mode when they are faced with reading questions. Asking for an active response, such as underlining and boxing details, will help them to pay more attention to the task.

Planning the Response

The planning stage may play out quite differently in different classrooms, depending on the test. I have actually heard teachers tell students who are about to take a timed test that they will not have time to plan a response but should just start writing as fast as they can. (This is one more reason why I am glad that my students do not face time restraints.) In other classrooms, all students must use a particular organizer or planning method.

The planning method I teach to students must meet several criteria. For one, it must be flexible enough to fit with many different kinds of questions. It must also be easy for students to remember. Finally, it must draw their attention to the text details that I want them to include in their responses.

As it turned out, my mother, Karen Pearce, had a simple yet efficient solution. She had taught her eighth graders the simple acronym *SEE* for *statement, examples, explanation*. Students could make a table with these headings and then write a general statement, include the specified number of text details, and explain how their details relate back to their answers. The labels explicitly cue them to include certain components of the answer.

Writing a Constructed Response

There are many times when you will have to write constructed responses to your reading. A constructed response can help you think about what you have read. It can give your teacher and others important information about your reading comprehension.

Think about a constructed response as your chance to show off your thinking. You want to prove how well you read and understand a text. You want to put your great ideas on paper.

But sometimes there's a problem between thinking great thoughts and putting those ideas on paper. Some constructed responses don't show great thinking. What are some common problems with short-answer responses?

Problems with Constructed Responses

To avoid these problems, follow some simple steps.

1. **Read the question carefully.** Underline the most important parts of the question. Put a box around the number of text details you are to include.
2. **Plan your response.** You may use an organizer to help you decide on the order of your details. This is the time to think about your answer and find the text details for support.
3. **Write your response.** Begin with a clear topic sentence that restates the question and states your answer clearly.
4. **Add your text details.** Be sure to write in complete sentences. Use the specific names of characters and places.
5. **Write a concluding sentence to wrap up your response.** Try to explain how your text details relate back to your answer.
6. **Proofread your response.** Did you answer the question? Did you include the correct number of text details?

Try it! A short-answer response question related to "Starting Out with Sled Dogs" is written below. We will work together to follow these steps to answer it.

> Would you like to own and train sled dogs? Why or why not? Support your response with at least three specific details from the text.

FIGURE 13–2.

I made a frame of this table as scaffolding for my neediest students (Figure 13–3). At first, I provided the statement and asked them to fill in the examples and explanation. As they became more comfortable with the process, they were able to take over control of the entire response. Throughout the process, I worked to ensure that students understood that the main goal was to answer the question, not to fill in all of the boxes on the organizer.

The SEE strategy works well for most kinds of questions except for summaries. I make sure that students know this, and I explain to them that they will need another planning tool for writing a summary.

Scoring Constructed Responses

Once students write their responses, it's time to score. Students need to see examples of responses at various levels, so I created a group activity that has them scoring multiple responses. I don't use individual student responses for this activity, because I don't want to embarrass students so early in the process. As they become more comfortable with one another and with writing constructed responses, they are better able to deal with peer criticism.

The sample responses in Figure 13–4 depict a range of the problems in student responses. The first response veers sharply off-topic, including far too much prior knowledge and not enough information from the text. The second one is fairly good, while the third one includes only one text detail.

I like to have students work in groups to score and discuss the samples (see Figure 13–5). Then, they score their own response. I often walk around the room and write my own score on students' papers so that they can see how their self-assessment matches with mine. When there are big discrepancies, I know that I need to give that student some individualized help.

Analyzing Students' Constructed-Response Questions

Once students have learned the basics of writing and scoring answers to constructed-response questions, I add them to my usual classroom instruction. Because I often have students working on multiple tasks at one time, I developed a generic scoring tool that includes a detailed analysis of responses (Figure 13–6). This tool has two parts. At the top, I can give a student a general score. Then, I use the grid on the bottom to analyze the errors in more depth. This makes scoring multiple responses fairly quick and easy. I can also pinpoint where students are having areas of difficulty and track their progress over time.

Conclusion

Helping students answer constructed-response questions is not easy. At one point, I thought that if I just taught students how to read well, they

Constructed Response Frame
SEE Organizer

Directions: The acronym *SEE* stands for *statement*, *examples*, and *explanation*. This is one way that you can remember what to put in your constructed responses.

Statement	I (would like, would not like) to own and train sled dogs.
Examples	Text example 1: Text example 2: Text example 3:
Explanation	(Explain how your examples relate back to your answer.)

FIGURE 13–3.

© 2008 by Emily Kissner from *The Forest and the Trees*. Portsmouth, NH: Heinemann.

Sample Constructed Responses

#1: I would love to have sled dogs. I think that dogs are really cute, and I know that I would take good care of them. I don't think that I would like to go out in the cold, though. Once I went on a winter camping trip and I didn't like it at all. Dogs have lots of fur to keep them warm, though.

#2: I would like to own sled dogs. I think it would be fun to take care of them and teach them how to pull a sled. I'd like to mow paths in the yard to teach them how to follow my commands. I think that I would like an Alaskan husky or a Malamute, because those sound like neat dogs.

#3: I wouldn't like to have sled dogs. I think it would be gross to give them water with meat juice!

FIGURE 13–4.

Constructed Response Scoring Activity

Score	Description
3	Demonstrates complete knowledge of the text. Three examples from the passage to support the explanation.
2	Demonstrates partial knowledge of the text. (Example: The student includes text details but does not explain how they support the answer.)
1	Demonstrates incomplete knowledge (Example: Student does not include specific examples from the text or includes wrong information from the text.)
0	Blank, off-topic, illegible.

Directions: Read each example your table has been given. Decide on a score for each one.

Example 1
Example 2
Example 3

Directions: Now, read your own response. Give yourself a score.

Your Score:
Explain the score you gave yourself.

_____

_____

_____

_____

_____

_____

FIGURE 13–5.

Scoring Constructed Responses

Score	Description
3	The reader answered the question using at least _____ specific text details. Details are accurate and clearly connect to the answer.
2	The reader answered the question using at least _____ specific text details. Details are mostly accurate and connect to the answer.
1	The reader answered the question, but no text details were used. *or* The reader answered the question, but text details reveal misinterpretation.
0	Incorrect, illegible, or off-topic response.

Analyzing Responses

	Interpreting the Question	Using Text Information	Drawing on Background Knowledge	Quality of Writing
	Misinterpreted function words (*why, what, where,* etc.) in question	Wrong information from the text is used to answer the question	Answer relies too much on prior knowledge at the expense of information from the text	Words in the answer seem to be mixed up or reversed
	Misinterpreted content words (specific to text) in question	Used information from a picture to answer the question	Answer does not reflect the reader's prior knowledge and inferences	Words used in the response are not precise; difficult to judge whether the answer is correct
	Answered only one part of the question	Used text information but not enough details	Prior knowledge is not integrated with new details	Answer seems correct, but not enough information is given
	Answer is obviously unrelated to the question			

FIGURE 13–6.

would naturally include the level of detail that is needed to answer these questions. Now I know that this is not the case. There are many readers who can but don't. When I teach them to consider the constructed response as a genre of writing with its own demands, then they begin to understand what is required.

As for Caleb—well, he brought me his reading assessment at the end of class. "It took me *twelve* lines to answer that question, Mrs. Kissner," he told me reproachfully. "Look at all the writing!"

Using Details for Constructed Response: What to Remember

- Most constructed-response questions require students to support their answers with details from the text.

- Writing skills do account for some measure of student performance on constructed-response questions.

- On a study of student responses to inference questions, responses often showed an overreliance on background knowledge.

- Other responses showed a lack of development.

- Students need to be taught if details are specific or not specific.

- Use organizers and acronyms with caution, as they may not be suited for all types of questions.

- Giving students the chance to score responses helps them look at responses critically and pinpoint problems.

14 THE PROFOUND EFFECT OF DETAILS

If there is anything that I've learned from studying the impacts of details in reading and writing, it is that the details of my classroom have a profound effect on my students. Everything is connected, from the message that greets students at the start of the day to the threads that carry us from one topic to another.

I have a new understanding of which details are important and which can be discarded. I'm not as interested in keeping up day by day with a prescribed list of objectives, but I'm more interested in understanding how students connect knowledge. I'm not as interested in knowing how many items students got correct, but I'm more interested in following their pathways to an answer. I'm less interested in knowing how many words a child can read per minute, but I'm more interested in listening to that child explain how they solve their reading problems. I don't care as much about who finished all five questions on the classwork as I do about what students will remember tomorrow, next week, next month.

Oh, I haven't conquered details. I still double and triple schedule myself, trying to cram more into one day than is humanly possible. I still forget to turn in paperwork and neglect to send my attendance down on time. Seductive details still pull my attention away from the big ideas. But learning more about details has given me a new respect for the way our brains work. The way that one detail can open up a wealth of background experiences, flood us with a tide of images, sounds, and smells, is remarkable. And our ability to integrate new details into existing schemas makes long-term learning possible.

As we look at the forests of main ideas, we also need to take some time to examine the individual trees—to think about why a particular tree may be growing in one particular way or how a grove of trees seems to thrive together. Just as every forest is made up of trees, every main idea is built of details—details that can open up a fascinating world of possibilities.

References

Albrecht, Jason, and Edward J. O'Brien. 1993. "Updating a Mental Model: Maintaining Both Local and Global Coherence." *Journal of Experimental Psychology: Learning, Memory, and Cognition* 19 (5): 1061–70.

Alexander, Joy. 2005. "The Verse-Novel: A New Genre." *Children's Literature in Education* 36 (3): 269–83.

Alverman, D., L. Smith, and J. Readence. 1985. "Prior Knowledge Activation and the Comprehension of Compatible and Incompatible Text." *Reading Research Quarterly* 20 (4): 420–36.

Bauer, Marion Dane. 1992. *What's Your Story? A Young Person's Guide to Writing Fiction*. New York: Clarion.

Bowyer-Crane, Claudine, and Margaret Snowling. 2005. "Assessing Children's Inference Generation: What Do Tests of Reading Comprehension Measure?" *British Journal of Educational Psychology* 75: 189–201.

Buckley, F. R. 1925 "Gold-Mounted Guns." In *American Short Stories*. Chicago: Scott, Foresman.

Cain, Kate, Jane Oakhill, and Peter Bryant. 2004. "Children's Reading Comprehension Ability: Concurrent Prediction by Working Memory, Verbal Ability, and Component Skills." *Journal of Educational Psychology* 96 (1): 31–42.

Cataldo, Maria, and Jane Oakhill. 2000. "Why Are Poor Comprehenders Inefficient Searchers? An Investigation into the Effects of Text Representation and Spatial Memory on the Ability to Locate Information in Text." *Journal of Educational Psychology* 92 (4): 791–9.

Coleman, Elaine, Ann Brown, and Inna Rivkin. 1997. "The Effects of Instructional Explanations on Learning from Scientific Texts." *The Journal of the Learning Sciences* 6 (4): 347–65.

Cote, Natalie. 1994. "Overcoming the Inert Knowledge Problem in Learning from Expository Text." Paper presented at the Annual Convention of the Mid-South Educational Research Association.

DiTerlizzi, Tony, and Holly Black. 2003. *The Field Guide*. New York: Simon and Schuster Books for Young Readers.

Durgunoglu, Aydin, and Jihn-Chang Jehng. 1991. Elaborative Inferences on an Expository Text. *Contemporary Educational Psychology* 16: 314–30.

Ericsson, K. Anders, and Walter Kintsch. 1995. "Long Term Working Memory." *Psychological Review* 102 (2): 211–45

Fincher-Kiefer, Rebecca, and Paul D'Agostino. 2004. "The Role of Visuospatial Resources in Generating Bridging and Predictive Inferences." *Discourse Processes* 37 (3) 205–224.

Fountas, Irene C., and Gay Su Pinnell. 2001. *Guiding Readers and Writers, Grades 3–6: Teaching Comprehension, Genre, and Content Literacy*. Portsmouth, NH: Heinemann.

Frost, Robert. 1923. "Nothing Gold Can Stay." In *The Yale Review v. 13 n. 1*. New Haven, CT: Yale University.

Gallini, Joan K., Hiller A. Spires, Suzanne Terry, and Jim Gleaton. 1993. "The Influence of Macro and Micro-Level Cognitive Strategies Training on Text Learning." *Journal of Research and Development in Education* 26 (3): 164–78.

Gambrell, Linda, and Ruby Bales. 1986. "Mental Imagery and the Comprehension-Monitoring Performance of Fourth- and Fifth-Grade Poor Readers." *Reading Research Quarterly* 21 (4): 454–64.

Garner, Ruth, Mark Gillingham, and C. Stephen White. 1989. "Effects of 'Seductive Details' on Macroprocessing and Microprocessing in Adults and Children." *Cognition and Instruction* 6 (1): 41–57.

Geiger, John, and Keith Millis. 2004. "Assessing the Impact of Reading Goals and Text Structures on Comprehension." *Reading Psychology* 25: 93–110.

George, Lindsay Barrett. 1995. *In the Woods: Who's Been Here?* New York: Greenwillow Books.

———. 1999. *Around the World: Who's Been Here?* New York: Greenwillow Books.

Goodman, Burton. 1990. *Surprises: 15 Great Stories with Surprise Endings*. Chicago: Jamestown.

Graesser, Arthur, Keith Millis, and Rolf Zwaan. 1997. "Discourse Comprehension." *Annual Review of Psychology* 48: 163–89.

Graesser, Arthur, Murray Singer, and Tom Trabasso. 1994. "Constructing Inferences During Narrative Text Comprehension." *Psychological Review* 101 (3): 371–95.

Hansen, Jane. 1981. "The Effects of Inference Training and Practice on Young Children's Reading Comprehension." *Reading Research Quarterly* 16 (3): 391–417.

Harlow, Joan Hiatt. 2005. *Midnight Rider*. New York: Margaret K. McElderry Books.

Harp, Shannon, and Amy Maslich. 2005. "The Consequences of Including Seductive Details During Lecture." *Teaching Psychology* 32 (2): 100–3.

Harvey, Stephanie, and Anne Goudvis. 2005. *The Comprehension Toolkit: Language and Lessons for Active Literacy*. Portsmouth, NH: Heinemann.

Hiaasen, Carl. 2002. *Hoot*. New York: Alfred A. Knopf.

Hunt, Irene. 1970. *No Promises in the Wind*. Chicago: Follett.

Jenkins, Joseph, Evelyn Johnson, and Jennifer Hileman. 2004. "When Is Reading Also Writing: Sources of Individual Differences in Performance on the New State Reading Assessments." *Scientific Studies of Reading* 8 (2): 125–51.

Kintsch, Eileen. 1990. "Macroprocesses and Microprocesses in the Development of Summarization Skill." *Cognition and Instruction* 7 (3): 161–95.

Kissner, Emily. 2006. *Summarizing, Paraphrasing, and Retelling: Skills for Better Reading, Writing, and Test Taking*. Portsmouth, NH: Heinemann.

Long, Debra, Mark Seely, and Brian Oppy. 1999. "The Strategic Nature of Less Skilled Readers' Suppression Problems." *Discourse Processes* 27 (3): 281–302.

MacHale, D. J. 2002. *Pendragon the Merchant of Death*. New York: Aladdin.

Mallat, Kathy. 2001. *Trouble on the Tracks*. New York: Walker and Company.

McCormick, Sandra. 1992. "Disabled Readers' Erroneous Responses to Inferential Comprehension Questions: Description and Analysis." *Reading Research Quarterly* 27 (1): 54–77.

McDonald, Megan. 2000. *Judy Moody*. Cambridge, MA: Candlewick Press.

McVee, Mary B., Kailonnie Dunmore, and James R. Gavelek. 2005. "Schema Theory Revisited." *Review of Educational Research* 75 (4): 531–566.

Nuthall, Graham. 1999a. "How Students Learn: The Validation of a Model of Knowledge Acquisition Using Stimulated Recall of the Learning Process." Paper presented at the Annual Meeting of the American Educational Research Association.

————. 1999b. "The Way Students Learn: Acquiring Knowledge from an Integrated Science and Social Studies Unit." *Elementary School Journal* 99: 303–41.

O'Brien, Robert. 1986. *Mrs. Frisby and the Rats of NIMH*. Fort Worth: Aladdin.

Peck, Richard. 1998. *A Long Way from Chicago: A Novel in Stories*. New York: Dial Books for Young Readers.

Perfetti, Charles, Nicole Landi, and Jane Oakhill. 2005. "The Acquisition of Reading Comprehension Skill." *The Science of Reading: A Handbook*, edited by M. J. Snowling and C. Hulme, 227–47. Oxford: Blackwell.

Posner, M. I., and S. E. Petersen. 1990. "The Attention System of the Human Brain." *Annual Review of Neuroscience* 13: 25–42.

Raphael, T., and P. D. Pearson. (1985). "Increasing Students' Awareness of Sources of Information for Answering Questions." *American Educational Research Journal* 22: 217–35.

Reiss, Kathryn. 1998. *PaperQuake: A Puzzle*. San Diego: Harcourt Brace.

Riordan, Rick. 2005. *The Lightning Thief*. New York: Miramax Books/ Hyperion Books for Children.

Rosenblatt, L. M. 1988. "Writing and Reading: The Transactional Theory." Technical Report No. 13. University of California at Berkeley and Carnegie Mellon University: Center for the Study of Writing.

Rowling, J. K. 1998. *Harry Potter and the Sorcerer's Stone*. New York: Arthur A. Levine Books.

————. 2000. *Harry Potter and the Goblet of Fire*. New York: Arthur A. Levine Books.

————. 2003. *Harry Potter and the Order of the Phoenix.* New York: Arthur A. Levine Books.

Sachar, Louis. 1987. *There's a Boy in the Girls' Bathroom.* New York: Knopf.

————. 2000. *Holes.* New York: Farrar, Straus and Giroux.

Schraw, Gregory, Suzanne Wade, and Carol Ann Kardash. 1993. "Interactive Effects of Text-Based and Task-Based Importance on Learning from Text." *Journal of Educational Psychology* 85 (4): 652–61.

Shank, Roger. 1979. "Interestingness: Controlling Inferences." *Artificial Intelligence* 12: 273–97.

Sousa, David. 2001. *How the Brain Learns.* Thousand Oaks, CA: Corwin Press.

Stahl, Steven, Michael Jacobson, Charlotte Davis, and Robin Davis. 1989. "Prior Knowledge and DifficultVocabulary in the Comprehension of Unfamiliar Text." *Reading Research Quarterly* 24 (1): 27–43.

Stewart, Paul, and Chris Riddell. 2004. *The Edge Chronicles: Beyond the Deepwoods.* Oxford, New York: David Fickling Books.

Sundbye, Nita. 1987. "Text Explicitness and Inferential Questioning: Effects on Story Understanding and Recall." *Reading Research Quarterly* 22 (1): 82–98.

Sylwester, Robert, and Joo-Yun Cho. 1992. "What Brain Research Says About Paying Attention." *Educational Leadership* 50: 71–5.

Therriault, David, and Gary Raney. 2002. "The Representation and Comprehension of Place-on-the-Page and Text-Sequence Memory." *Scientific Studies of Reading* 6 (2): 117–34.

Tolkien, J. R. R. 1965. *The Lord of the Rings.* Boston: Houghton Mifflin.

Tomlinson, Louise. 1995. "Flag Words for Efficient Thinking, Active Reading, Comprehension, and Test Taking." *Journal of Reading* 38 (5): 387–8.

Van Allsburg, Chris. 1986. *The Stranger.* Boston: Houghton Mifflin.

van Dijk, T. A., and W. Kintsch. 1983. *Strategies of Discourse Comprehension.* New York: Academic Press.

Wade, Suzanne, Gregory Schraw, William Buxton, and Michael Hayes. 1993. "Seduction of the Strategic Reader: Effects of Interest on

Strategies and Recall." *Reading Research Quarterly* 28 (2): 92–114.

Walczyk, Jeffrey. 2000. "The Interplay Between Automatic and Control Processes in Reading." *Reading Research Quarterly* 35 (4): 554–66.

Walczyk, Jeffrey, Cheryl Marsiglia, Amanda Johns, and Keli Bryan. 2004. "Children's Compensations for Poorly Automated Reading Skills" *Discourse Processes* 37 (1): 47–66.

Walczyk, Jeffrey, and Diana A. Griffith-Ross. 2007. "How Important Is Reading Skill Fluency for Comprehension?" *The Reading Teacher* 60 (6): 560–9.

Weaver, C. A., and W. Kintsch. 1991. "Expository Text." *Handbook of Reading Research*, Vol. 2, edited by R. Barr, M. L. Kamil, P. B. Mosenthal, and P. D. Pearson, 230–45. New York: Longman.

Wells, Rosemary. 2007. *Red Moon at Sharpsburg: A Novel*. New York: Viking.

Wilder, Laura Ingalls. 1935. *Little House on the Prairie*. New York: Harper.

Willoughby, Teena, Eileen Wood, Serge Desmarais, Suzanne Sims, and Michelle Kalra. 1997. "Mechanisms That Support the Effectiveness of Elaboration Strategies." *Journal of Educational Psychology* 89 (4): 682–5.

Wilson, Leslie Owen. 1998. "The Eighth Intelligence: Naturalistic Intelligence." *New Horizons for Learning Electronic Journal* 3 (5). Available at: www.newhorizons.org/journal/journal17.htm.

Winne, Philip, Lorraine Graham, and Leone Prock. 1993. "A Model of Poor Readers' Text-Based Inferencing: Effects of Explanatory Feedback." *Reading Research Quarterly* 28 (1): 52–66.

Yarlas, Aaron. 1999. "Schema Modification and Enhancement as Predictors of Interest: A Test of the Knowledge-Schema Theory of Cognitive Interest." Paper presented at the Annual Meeting of the American Educational Research Association. Montreal, Canada, April 19–23, 1999.